Light
in a
Dark
Place

"The Story of Chicago's Oldest Rescue Mission"

by Ralph Woodworth

Light and Life Press
Winona Lake, Indiana 46590

Printed in the United States of America
by Light and Life Press
Winona Lake, Indiana
46590

ISBN 0-89367-022-7

To My Mother
Naomi Males Woodworth

Preface

This is the story of the oldest rescue mission in Chicago — Olive Branch Mission. But a mission, an institution, has no history apart from the people involved in it. So, this account is an attempt to set forth the mission through the dreams and failures, laughter and tears, prayers and victories of mission workers, converts, and friends.

But of the thousands of people associated with the mission during its first one hundred one years, only a small fraction are even named in these pages. The unnamed workers and friends are no less important to the mission, nor are the converts whose stories are omitted any less dramatic.

Only God's account books can give an accurate record of all the good done through this lighthouse on skid row. And those books are not yet open to us. Until they are, any other account must leave out much more than is ever included.

Table of Contents

Date List

1876   Rachael Bradley starts sewing class
1883   Wells Street Mission opens
1890   Mary J. Everhart arrives
1891   Mission moves to 95 S. Desplaines and is renamed Olive Branch
1893   Rachael Bradley dies
1893   Mission reopened by Mary J. Everhart, with Lulu Howe
1894   *Olive Branch* paper started
1895   Katie V. Hall arrives
1896   Incorporation
1902   Mission workers' home purchased at 114 S. Peoria Street
1902   Mabel E. Lane arrives
1905   Clara B. Spencer arrives
1911   Mission workers' home moved to 2034 W. Monroe Street
1927   Mission moved to 1047 W. Madison Street
1928   Mary J. Everhart dies
1928   Mabel E. Lane becomes superintendent
1930   Olive Branch Training School opens

1933 Martha Boots arrives
1939 Mabel E. Lane dies
1939 Katie V. Hall becomes superintendent
1949 Building at 1051 W. Madison Street purchased
1952 Katie V. Hall dies
1952 Martha Boots becomes superintendent
1953 Clara B. Spencer dies
1954 C. N. Schumaker becomes superintendent
1956 Monroe Street mission workers' home sold
1958 Christian Shelter opens
1963 Christian Shelter destroyed by fire
1967 Alice Schumaker dies
1968 C. N. Schumaker retires
1969 K. K. Ballenger becomes director
1969 Olive Branch Training School closed
1970 *Olive Branch* paper replaced by newsletter
1974 K. K. Ballenger retires
1974 H. T. Rasche becomes director
1976 Centennial Observance

Chapter 1

Stepmother of a Mission

"Oh, boys, you shouldn't be doing that!"

Three grimy little fellows looked up from the dust of the alley. They stared at the slight woman leaning out the window.

"What's that, ma'am?" the shabbiest one asked in pretended innocence.

"You boys shouldn't be drinking that vile poison. Don't you see what it does to the men and women all up and down this street?"

"Yes, ma'am. But you see, ma'am, we were thirsty; and we only had a nickel among us." The spokesman picked up the pail of beer and led his partners away from the reproachful gaze of Miss Everhart.

Mary Everhart's interest in the three boys was not just a momentary one. She had come from Pennsylvania six years before to teach in the Chicago Industrial Home for Children. Two months later she was helping Mrs. Rachael Bradley in the Wells Street Mission.

Within two and a half years, Mrs Bradley was taken home to heaven, and Mary found herself with the full responsibility for the mission. Day after weary day, she worked to turn people from alcohol, tobacco, drugs, and prostitution to follow the better way of Jesus Christ. But one of her greatest concerns was to keep the children of the slums from following the bad example of the adults in their world.

Mary Everhart was born on a farm near Lickingville, Pennsylvania, on February 13, 1853, the granddaughter of a Scotch Methodist preacher. She was an only child. Perhaps that helps account for the loving relationship between Mary and her parents. Still, she grew up with a strong determination to plot her own course in life. She wanted to teach school, a job her father considered a part of the man's world. But with his grudging consent, she set out on that career while still in her teens.

By the time Mary moved to Chicago, she had been a teacher for twenty years. Along the way she had graduated from the normal school in Edinboro, Pennsylvania. Her accomplishments had given her a distinct sense of pride and a love for the finer things of life, especially nice clothes.

Mary certainly did not anticipate getting involved in mission work when she moved to Chicago. Of course, she was concerned for the spiritual welfare of others. She often took time to pray with students. But she was a teacher; that was all.

It was T. B. Arnold, the superintendent of the Chicago Industrial Home for Children, who first detected her potential for mission work. She protested her unworthiness. But finally, after much persuasion, she consented to help Rachael Bradley. Her first day in the mission was Christmas Day 1891 — the busiest day of the year.

Before Mary agreed to succeed Mrs. Bradley as the leader of the mission, she had a clear call from God. It came one day while she was struggling in prayer. Sick of the sights and sounds and smells of the slums, she cried, "Let me return home to Pennsylvania." God's response was, "You have no home this side of the river." When she accepted God's call, she never looked back.

It may be that the character of Rachael Bradley helped to draw Mary into mission work. Mrs. Bradley also had been a very proud woman. In her pre-mission days she had been described as a "tall, queenly-looking woman." She, too, had loved fine clothing. But when the power of God filled her, she was changed totally. From that time on, she didn't care about her own comforts. All her efforts were directed toward serving the poor and needy in Jesus' name.

It was in 1876 that Rachael Bradley started a sewing class for the poor. She held this in her church, the Morgan Street Free Methodist Church, every Saturday. But the class did not provide enough opportunity to minister to others. She began to look for a hall in which she could open a mission. Her pastor tried to dissuade her from that dream, pleading the lack of money and predicting certain failure. But as soon as she located an old hall on Wells Street on Chicago's near northside, the mission became a reality.

There was only one large room in the hall which had to serve for both mission and living quarters. A curtain provided the only separation between the two. For sixteen years, by word and deed, Rachael Bradley preached the love of God in the heart of Chicago's slums. Death came prematurely, hurried on no doubt by the awful conditions of her voluntary exile.

When Mary Everhart found Rachael Bradley, the older woman was very sick. Mary nursed her back to some measure of health, and together they carried on the work.

The mission was moved to South Desplaines Street in 1891. Of course, the change of location demanded a change of name. After much prayer, Rachael Bradley chose Olive Branch Mission as the most appropriate.

Two years later Mrs. Bradley again fell ill, and it became all but certain she would not live. In preparation for death, she sold all the mission equipment to Mary. In that way, Mary became the owner-superintendent of the mission. Mary would sell the equipment back to Mrs. Bradley at the purchase price, if she recovered.

The mission remained closed for several weeks after Rachael Bradley's death. Then Mary, along with Lulu Howe, determined to resume the work. The mission was reopened on August 30, 1893. Mary picked up the reins of leadership and did not let them go until her death thirty-five years later. She proved to be a strong, resourceful, energetic, yet sympathetic leader who relied fully upon God.

For nearly a year Mary and Lulu lived in the ten-by-twelve-foot room curtained off at the back of the Desplaines Street mission hall. A kindly policeman warned them repeatedly about the danger of two women living alone in such a neighborhood. But they happily confessed their confidence in the power of God, and stayed. (The policeman was killed in the line of duty several years later.) They stayed — because there was not money enough to rent both a mission hall and an apartment. So, for the time being, the living quarters would have to wait. As it was, Mary had to pay many of the mission expenses from her own pocket.

The mission hall had been a chicken coop, and, before that, a saloon. The landlord cleaned it up, after a fashion, and the ladies decorated the walls with Scripture quotations It was in a rickety old building which was in danger of being condemned by the city health department. Several years later all but the first floor was condemned. Ten or twelve families lived in the three-story building where privacy was almost nonexistent. Rats often crawled into the most inaccessible spaces between the walls and died. The resulting odor was impossible to eliminate. Burning apple parings helped, but not much.

Saloons, gambling dens, and houses of prostitution abounded. At one time, there were thirteen saloons in the block in which the mission was located and a total of three hundred thirty-seven within three-quarters of a mile. The mission workers moved into the Green Street Rescue Home in 1896 to operate it for two years. To their dismay, they discovered that every house on the block, except theirs, was a house of prostitution.

Mary and her band of mission workers moved from place to place for years. They often turned away willing workers because of the lack of housing.

At a camp meeting in Bowling Green, Ohio, in 1895, Mary told about her work. W. B. Olmstead took an offering on behalf of the mission. To his surprise, and Mary's, it totaled $311.43. Of course, the money was needed for current expenses. But after much prayer, Mary decided to use it to start a fund for the purchase of a home for the mission workers. After seven years, they were able to buy a house at 114 South Peoria Street. There they lived for nine years, when they moved into a better house at 2034 West Monroe Street.

About two years after Mary and Lulu reopened the mission, Lulu married Martin Hansen. The newlyweds went to live in Evanston, Illinois. Only weeks earlier, another worker had come to Olive Branch. Katie V. Hall would give fifty-seven years of service to the work. In the next ten years, three other young women joined Mary in the work of reclaiming lost men and women in Chicago's slums: Mabel E. Lane, Delia Darling, and Clara B. Spencer. These, along with Mary and Katie, provided the backbone of the mission staff for nearly sixty years.

A typical week provided Mary with many opportunities for ministry. First, there were the evangelistic services every evening. The workers and converts met at the mission at 7:00 P.M. for a time of prayer. Then they walked a half-block up the street to the corner of Madison and Desplaines for an open air meeting, weather permitting. Following that meeting, people were invited to the mission hall for the indoor service. The workers always gave an altar invitation, and usually there was at least one hungry soul with whom to pray. These services often lasted until 11:00 or later.

Each Wednesday afternoon the workers visited in the Cook County Hospital for several hours. Sunday mornings they conducted services in the neighborhood police station. On the way home, they would hold another service in the lodging house on Green Street. Sunday afternoon there was Sunday school for both children and adults. Then there was the converts' meeting, where those who had accepted Christ received spiritual help and were encouraged to press on in their Christian experience. These were followed by the evening street meeting and evangelistic service.

In addition to the set services, there was always much visitation in homes, lodging houses, and saloons. There was food and clothing to distribute. They must prepare and mail the *Olive Branch* paper. And there was always a great pile of unanswered letters clamoring for attention. All this was in addition to meal preparation, house cleaning, laundry, and other household tasks.

In the thirty-five years that Mary Everhart was superintendent of the mission, conversions averaged one a day. She saw her primary task as soul-winning. Physical needs were an ever-present concern and took much of her time and energy; but she viewed them as secondary to winning the lost to Christ.

Chapter 2

In the Highways

"He's dead!"

"He's killed him!"

The drunken victor staggered away through the crowd, leaving his equally drunken opponent lying lifeless upon the street.

Someone ran for a glass of water. Another rushed to the drugstore for help. A third went to call an ambulance. Mary Everhart and her workers and converts offered a brief prayer for the safety of the victim, assured themselves that he was not seriously injured, and resumed the street meeting.

The interruption was unplanned, but it certainly was not unexpected as far as Mary was concerned. When she had initiated the street meetings, she knew the services would not be carefully ordered as in a peaceful country church. The deft way in which she handled a variety of emergencies revealed her confidence in God as well as her determination to do His will.

The plan for a street meeting was always the same. Some of the workers and converts would pray together for about thirty minutes. Others made the rounds of the nearby saloons with personal invitations to the meeting. Then they assembled a half block away from the mission hall on the corner of Madison and Desplaines. There they formed a half circle, the men on one side, the women on the other. They stood in the street facing the sidewalk where the audience could congregate. Later, a city ordinance compelled them to stay out of the street.

Music was the drawing card. As the missionaries lifted their voices in song, some using megaphones, the idlers along the streets in all directions would drift within hearing range. When a crowd had assembled, the converts and workers began giving their testimonies of how God had saved them from a life of sin. Then one of the workers or a visiting minister or mature Christian layman would give a brief gospel message. The workers then invited everyone to the hall for the continuance of the meeting. That was the plan. Sometimes it worked out that way; often it didn't.

One evening, just as the street meeting was getting well started, the windows of the three-story lodging house on that corner were thrown open. Great billows of thick sulfur smoke came pouring out. Mission workers and converts choked, coughed, and wiped away their tears as the crowd fled. No, the house had not caught fire. The landlord had been fumigating the house that day and had decided to release the noxious fumes at that strategic moment. When the air cleared, the meeting was resumed.

That same evening the singing was accompanied by the enthusiastic beat of a large, well-dressed, drunken man. His antics lent a circus atmosphere to the music, but they did not defeat the purpose of the meeting. Before it was concluded, more than a half dozen men sought the Lord for the forgiveness of sins.

Mary Everhart and her band held a meeting at the corner of Madison and Desplaines nearly every evening, weather permitting, for the thirty-five years of her superintendency. But their right to the corner did not always go unchallenged. One night they found their place occupied by a Socialist soapbox orator. He refused to budge, and so they moved a block further down Madison Street. The crowd was slow to gather, and it never got as large as they had come to expect at their usual corner. The noise from the neighboring saloons and passing wagons and streetcars, coupled with the smallness of their group, kept their spirits from rising very high.

After more than an hour, they trudged back to the mission hall, too discouraged and tired to try to hold a preaching service. Instead, they went to prayer. As they prayed, a clean-cut young man at one side of the room rose and said, "I want you to pray for me."

They were glad to grant his request. He prayed, too. But at first his prayer was completely without believing faith. He had been living an on-again-off-again experience with God for about two years. By his own confession, he had been in sin more than he had been trying to please God. As he prayed and they prayed, faith began to come. After a long time, he claimed the victory in Jesus' name; and in the days to follow, he demonstrated a truly changed life.

The struggle with the Socialists for possession of the corner of Madison and Desplaines continued for years. One February evening in 1913, the Socialists were already

19

speaking when the mission workers arrived. Mary and the converts and workers simply began as though there was not another meeting in progress. Soon the mission workers had the largest part of the crowd. This enraged the Socialists. They began hurling outrageously insulting remarks at the Christians. Their behavior grew more obnoxious and boisterous until Mary sent for the police.

The officers marched two of the Socialist leaders off to the stationhouse, and the others followed to see what would happen. But before the street meeting ended, the Socialists were back interrupting the speaker and thrusting handbills into any hand. One even stuffed a piece of literature down Katie Hall's megaphone, hoping to silence her persistent voice.

The next evening the Socialists were again in place when the mission workers arrived on the disputed corner. One of the converts stepped forward and said, "Excuse me, gentlemen, this is my corner for a gospel service."

His claim brought only scorn from the Socialists. At this, the convert raised his trumpet-like voice and began sounding out his testimony. He told how God had saved him from a wretched condition more than two years before. He was still praising Jesus when the Socialists started down Madison Street shouting "Rats! Rats! Rats!" as they went. With that, the sympathy of the crowd shifted completely to the Christians, and a good meeting followed.

Socialists were not the only ones who wished to capture the audience at the corner of Madison and Desplaines. At least one time there were four street meetings in progress at that intersection at the same time. Besides the Socialists and the Olive Branch workers, there were groups from two other missions, one of which used a big bass drum. Each group had a corner, and the crowd took its pick. One well-dressed young man chose the Olive Branch group, and he was saved that night.

It was Mary's plan to use the street meeting to attract

a crowd and interest them in the gospel. Then she could invite them into the mission hall for serious spiritual work. But sometimes things moved faster than that. One evening a drunken man fell to his knees, bowed at the curb, and began to cry to God for mercy. Soon another man was upon his knees. The mission workers and converts gathered around and began to pray with the seekers and point them to Christ.

The throng that had come to be entertained found this development very interesting. They crowded next to the praying missionaries to better hear and see what was happening. As the seekers each broke through to spiritual victory, they jumped to their feet and began to testify and exhort the gaping listeners. Many jammed into the mission hall that night and many found deliverance from sin. The meeting which had begun on the street at 7:30 concluded near midnight.

In 1920, the Eighteenth Amendment went into effect. Thus the manufacture, sale, or transportation of intoxicating beverages became illegal. That law should have changed the environment of the mission neighborhood. But the change was only superficial, for illegal booze was still readily available.

One evening Mary spied a woman approaching the street meeting with a sheet of paper in her hand. She was going from one man to another speaking to them and apparently asking them to sign the paper. Upon investigation, Mary discovered that the paper was a petition to allow certain types of intoxicating beverages. Indignantly, Mary began to warn the woman about the evil she was doing. To Mary, the strongest argument for prohibition was the thousands of men whose lives had been destroyed by beverage alcohol.

It was always hard to anticipate what might come down the street next. One evening the meeting was temporarily broken up when a crew of street sweepers approached. They drove debris before them with their push brooms and raised a choking cloud of dust. One of the workers capitalized upon that situation by exhorting the crowd to seek cleanness of heart. Often the meeting was disintegrated by a passing parade, complete with marching bands. On such occasions the missionaries and converts waited out the distraction and then started afresh.

The men who came to listen at the street meetings did not always do so out of spiritual hunger. Often they came to jeer the converts. One fellow who had well earned the nickname "Old Drunken Taylor" was saved at the mission. Four months later, while he was giving his testimony on the street, a voice from the crowd accused, "You was drunk three weeks ago!" The speaker pushed right ahead with his witness. Another new Christian was interrupted with the words, "You stole my coat!" The babe in Christ paid no heed to the false accusation, but went right on telling about what Christ had done for him.

Mary Everhart was never bashful about pressing visiting ministers into service. One such visitor was the Reverend W. H. Coffee. He came to Chicago in October of 1917 to visit the Free Methodist Publishing House. One evening, President Woodrow Wilson was to speak at the Stock Yards Auditorium. Many from the publishing house had been invited and promised seats on the platform. They urged Mr. Coffee to accompany them. He was waiting in line with them when he decided that the crowd was too great for the hall. So, he left to visit Olive Branch Mission and his wife's friend, Mary Everhart.

As he turned the corner from Madison Street onto Desplaines, bound for the mission, Mr. Coffee entered bedlam. There were hundreds of drunk people. They were quarreling, shoving, begging, cursing, mocking. Some sang ribald songs to gospel hymn tunes. Amid all the confusion, one man half-lay, half-sat against a building with his hat pulled down over his eyes. In the middle of the block, Mr. Coffee came upon Mary and her workers and converts just starting out for the nightly street meeting. He reports, "When she saw me she thought she had found a sacrifice caught by the horns in the thicket and immediately announced that I would preach that evening."

Mr. Coffee accompanied the missionaries back toward the corner of Madison Street. As they passed the man lying against the building, another man came along and kicked him and waited to see if he was dead or alive. Finding him dead, he went on his way. Mary explained that the man had been lying there about two hours. The police had been notified but had not yet arrived.

The band of missionaries took up their position opposite the Socialists and began to sing. Suddenly, the window of the saloon across the street was shattered by a brickbat. The culprit fled down the street, leaping over the corpse on the sidewalk, with the howling mob from the saloon close on his heels. They caught him and dragged him back to the scene of the crime. Inside, they set about discussing their differences in the noisiest way possible.

Through all the confusion, the mission band sang, prayed, testified, and exhorted. When the service moved indoors, some seekers followed. At least one young man found Christ as Saviour that night. W. H. Coffee claimed that he had made a good exchange when he traded hearing an address by the president of the United States for the opportunity to see God work in the slums of Chicago.

Bishop Walter A. Sellew was a frequent speaker at the mission. This is how he evaluated the street meetings:

"When it is understood that these meetings are conducted in the slum district of Chicago, where the vilest and most degraded people in this country congregate, some idea may be had of the troubles that constantly beset these workers. If one drunken man disturbs them, there is sure to be another there, equally drunk, to defend them. These meetings are very interesting, instructive, and unique. Frequently, fine, intelligent, and reputable people who are passing become interested and stop and listen. The testimonies of the converts are always interesting and sometimes actually thrilling. I was so impressed by them that I hesitated about speaking myself, because it did not seem to me, after having heard the testimonies of these converts, that what I would say would interest the crowd.''

Chapter 3

God's Workshop

"Let me go, Lady."

"Amen."

"Lady, please let me go."

"Amen."

"I'll come back tomorrow evening and get saved."

"Amen," Mary repeated yet again, without budging from her place before the door.

The unkempt young man looked down at the gentle face before him. Somehow this mission lady reminded him of his mother. His eyes began to mist and his lips trembled. Then she had him by the elbow, directing him toward the makeshift altar at the front of the room. Before long he was up from his knees, praising God for the deliverance from sins and thanking those who had prayed with him.

The men who came into Olive Branch Mission were from widely different backgrounds. They were of different nationalities, different social strata, and different educational opportunities. But they had one thing in common — they were all undone by sin. And 90 percent of them were slaves of alcohol.

A woman working with such men had to deal firmly with them. One time as the altar call was being given, a finely dressed young man dashed toward the door. Mary met him in the aisle. She stopped his flight, turned him toward the altar, and bid him seek God. He did and found wonderful deliverance.

Another evening after the service had started, a young workingman entered the hall. He walked deliberately to the stove where he knocked the ashes from his cigar and took a seat near the front. His manner warned the mission workers and converts that he was not to be bullied. But several began praying for him, and some even dared to speak to him of his need of Christ. Within little more than an hour, this hostile young man had become one with the Christians, giving praise to the God who can forgive sins.

Another regular guest speaker was Auntie Cooke. It was this same Sarah Anne Cooke who had been instrumental in guiding D. L. Moody into the fullness of the Holy Spirit in 1871. The evangelist was an active man, and his activity had accomplished great things. But those results were nothing compared to what God could do through him. Auntie Cooke and a friend covenanted to pray for Moody. When they informed him of their intention, he was flabbergasted. But they kept at it.

Finally, he invited them to his room to pray with him each Friday afternoon as he began seeking the blessing of which they witnessed. Moody struggled for months. When the Spirit of God came in fullness, Moody became a different man. Before, he had thought of Auntie Cooke and her friend as "those two dreadful women." Now they were "those two wonderful women." Auntie Cooke, a Free Methodist, made it a practice to visit a different gospel service every night of the week. For years, Olive Branch was on her circuit.

The sermons preached in the mission were always simple and direct. They always called for a commitment on the part of the hearers. Mary and her workers did much of the preaching, but with a service every evening of the year, they were glad to utilize the help of guest preachers. The Reverend W. B. Olmstead was one of the regular guests. He was there for the last week of the year 1895. During those seven days, the crowd averaged about two hundred twenty-five per service. There were seekers in every service but one. As many as twenty-five asked for prayer during a single service.

The preaching usually took the form of straight Bible exposition and exhortation to seek God. Very little was said about specific sins such as the use of whiskey and tobacco. Nevertheless, those who sought God seemed to know they could not receive God and keep their former vices. One seeker stopped praying long enough to draw a handful of cigars from an inner pocket and hurl them to the floor. Then he found freedom to pray on God's terms. Many a poor fellow fueled the old mission stove from the contents of his pockets. And the kitchen sink was well preserved from freezing by the quantity of alcohol dumped down the drain.

Many evenings, Mary sat beside a drunken man to prevent him from disturbing the service. She did not like to put anyone out of the service, because her goal was to see them delivered from sin. But when necessity demanded, she would march even the biggest drunk right out the door.

Because the congregation was made up largely of drunks, certain precautions had to be taken. When a seeker went to the altar, he had to take his hat and other belongings with him, or they might be stolen while he prayed. One time the precaution was overlooked, and a seeker lost a brand-new pair of shoes. Mary's motto became Watch and Pray.

One rainy October evening a little group of workers and converts huddled in the mission hall for what promised to be a rather uneventful meeting. A few men came in from the street in response to the singing. Then one after another, the converts gave testimony of what God had done and was doing for them. When it was nearly time for the speaker to begin, a young man rose near the door and asked permission to sing a song his father had taught him. "I am not a Christian," he said, "and I do not want to disturb your meeting. But will you care if I sing this song?"

Mary made sure that the song was a Christian one and then gave him permission to sing. When he had finished the song, he told his story. "I have served time in prison twice. Once I was a prisoner three years. Not long ago I was arrested and charged with grand larceny. I prayed and told the Lord that if He would let me off with an easy sentence, I would serve Him. I was sentenced for only six months.

"Last night," he continued, "I was attracted by your singing, and as I listened, God talked to my heart. I went into that saloon on the corner, and while I sat there drinking a glass of whiskey and thinking over my past life, I longed to be free from sin. I started to go to the meeting again, but the meeting was gone and I did not know where to find it. Tonight I heard the singing here at the door, and I thought this must be the meeting I lost last night, so I came down. From tonight on, I expect to live a better life."

A few minutes later, as the message was being given, the young man got to his feet and left the hall. Later, during the season of prayer, Mary and the others prayed specifically for him. As they prayed, he returned to the hall. He accepted the invitation to seek God and soon found the peace he so desired.

Every service in the mission concluded with a season of prayer. An invitation would be given for people to seek God. Often some would respond at the general invitation. While some Christians prayed with those who had come, others would walk through the crowd speaking to hesitant ones. One evening Mary approached a well-dressed, intelligent-looking man who had come in late and was seated near the door. "Are you a Christian?" she asked.

"I do not claim to be," he replied, "but I am perfectly satisfied just the way I am."

Mary made no verbal response, but she looked him steadily in the eye.

"You question my word?" he demanded.

"I do not understand how you can feel that way," she explained, "since only God's children are truly satisfied."

"But I am satisfied," he repeated with emphasis.

"Well, God can do nothing for you while you are in that state of mind."

Mary gave him an invitation to return to the mission services. And she determined to pray for him.

He came back night after night. He seemed increasingly unsatisfied with himself but still unwilling to yield to God. Then one evening he asked Mary, "Did I understand you to say the other night that a good moral man would stand no better chance than these wrecks of humanity?"

"Yes," she replied, "as far as meriting the favor of God and getting to heaven by your good works. Socially you are far better, but you self-sufficient, self-satisfied moralists are farther from the kingdom than these poor

29

drunkards — 'The publicans and the harlots go into the kingdom of God before you.' "

To her fresh urging that he seek God, he only replied, "No, I am doing the best I know how, and I think I am all right."

Mary noticed that each evening he was seated a little nearer to the front of the hall. One evening he listened eagerly to the testimony of a young convert. The new Christian told how God had saved him from a life of awful sin and given him power to witness freely. The moralist said, "This young man has something I don't have."

When he was invited to the altar for prayer that evening, he objected, "It will do me no good," and started for the door. But one of the converts who had taken an interest in him had snatched up his hat and overcoat, carried them to the front, and laid them on the altar. The moralist hestitated, but then moved to the altar where he knelt beside his garments while others prayed for him. He complained he could not pray because there seemed to be a great mountain before him. As others prayed, gradually the mountain dissolved and he began to seek God. Soon victory came and he was relieved of his awful load of sin and guilt.

Sometimes Mary Everhart and Olive Branch Mission were only part of the instrumentality of God in bringing salvation to some lost soul. One whose search ended at Olive Branch was a young Jewish man. He had been coming to the services for several nights and had asked for and received a Bible. Mary felt that God was speaking to him and that he ought to yield.

"I can't; I have too much to give up," he said. Then he hurried on to explain that he did not mean pleasure or worldly attractions, but his people. He had been raised in a strict Jewish home and designated by his father to be educated as a rabbi. He had been sent to seminary in Cincinnati. While there, he discovered the New Testament. Through his reading of that book, he became convinced that Jesus of Nazareth is the Messiah. When his discovery became known, he was expelled from the school and cut off from all his Jewish friends and associates as a heretic. For two and a half years he had been struggling with the knowledge of Jesus without having the peace which He affords.

After Mary spoke to the young Jew that night, several others did too. But he put off each appeal and moved closer to the door. Finally, at the very threshold, a convert convinced him to seek God. They knelt at the altar while others gathered around to help with the praying.

When he met God's terms, he jumped to his feet in an ecstasy of joy. He threw his arms around the fellow who had brought him to the altar. Then, rubbing his hands together, he exclaimed, "It is inexpressible!" He laid his hand over his heart and said, "There is some load gone!"

Not all who knelt at that altar were men. Women bowed there, too. One who came seemed a bird of paradise next to the shabby starlings who knelt near her. There were six brightly colored feathers in the hat set upon properly coiffured hair. White linen cuffs drew one's attention toward the hands where diamond rings sparkled. How did such a one find her way to the altar of a slum mission?

Della had grown up in the home of an infidel saloonkeeper. She ran away from home as a young teen and made her life in several different houses of prostitution. When she heard that her younger sister was ill, she contacted her parents and persuaded them to place the sister in her care. Of course, Della didn't want to bring her innocent sister into a house of shame; so she managed to place her in a Christian home. This contact with and care for a sister started Della's life in a new direction.

She grew progressively sick of her life of sin until she landed in a home conducted by the Olive Branch Mission workers. Della thought she was there only to be

31

rehabilitated and trained for some kind of employment. But the mission workers knew she was there to find God.

One of the other girls in the home told Della what God had done for her and persuaded Della to attend the services in the mission. When the altar call was given, Della thought it was hilarious that anyone would expect a person to kneel at an altar constructed of chairs and pray aloud. But much to her surprise, several men promptly responded. Della watched this spectacle night after night. Then one Sunday evening, she joined the group at the altar and asked Jesus Christ to come into her heart and make her clean.

God answered her prayer, and Della went out to live the new life in Jesus Christ.

Chapter 4

Treasure Hunting

"Oh, just one, please. Just one!" cried the white-haired old woman as she stretched out her hand toward the dwindling supply of fresh peaches.

Mary had started this day's outing to the poorhouse with high expectations. The mission had received a generous supply of the luscious fruit from country friends. Mary and her staff had immensely enjoyed the treat and had willingly shared it with their neighbors. Then at ten o'clock this morning they had set out for Dunning, loaded

with tracts, papers, and peaches. At Mary's suggestion,
they first visited the children's ward. There they watched
with delight as each pair of little hands grasped a peach.
But as they advanced from ward to ward, they soon were
dismayed to find their supplies woefully short of the
demand. Now they had only a few pieces of fruit left. They
determined to give them only to the sick.

Mary delighted to share her treats with the poor
around her. She often carried flowers to the hospital,
when she could get them. She discovered that a bouquet of
flowers could gladden many hearts when it was taken
apart and given away, one flower at a time.

The day Mary met Willie she didn't have flowers with
her. But she did have some Sunday school papers. Willie
took the paper gladly, and read it. He was only a boy, but
he had been in the hospital for eighteen months. His
bright, cheery smile lifted the spirits of many as he rode
around the ward in his wheelchair. Mary visited Willie
week after week and prayed for him. Finally, she
persuaded him to pray for himself.

Willie enjoyed reading the papers Mary left with him.
He began reading the New Testament. One day when
Mary came, Willie seemed extra cheerful. "Do you know
why?" he asked. "Because I prayed, and God took away
the pain and let me go to sleep." It was the first pain-free
night he had experienced in more than three months.
When Mary came the next week, Willie had gone to be
with Jesus.

Another little fellow Mary met was in much worse
circumstances than Willie — he was in the police station
jail. His mother had been locked up to await trial, and he,
having no place else to go, was there with her. His case
was not so very extreme, for Mary found all kinds of
people there. Since the inmates of the police station jail
were simply awaiting trial, Mary rarely saw an individual
there two weeks in a row.

The mission workers visited the police station every

Sunday morning. The jail was in the basement. It consisted of three corridors with cells along each corridor. The floors, ceiling, and three walls were made of stone. The fourth wall consisted of one-inch iron bars set about two inches apart. As Mary and her helpers stood on one side of the iron bars singing, preaching, testifying, and praying, the inmates on the other side of the bars laughed, cried, slept, listened, jeered, or continued with their card game. No task was more difficult than conducting a service under such circumstances. But Mary was sure that the seed sown there would bear fruit, and it did.

One Sunday a young man wept bitter tears of remorse for his wasted life and his present condition. As the mission workers prepared to leave, he drew from his pocket his last two cents and insisted that they take them.

Another time, as they started to sing, they were joined by a deep rich voice far back in the corridor. When they could see who was singing, they found a portly, well-dressed, elderly man. He requested that they sing the "old" songs; and as they did, he sang along with tears marking his face. He had been a Christian and the superintendent of a large Sunday school before sin had dragged him down.

A rough-looking young Polish man seemed to get some help one Sunday. The following evening he appeared at the mission. But his appearance was so changed that he had to explain that he was the one with whom they had prayed the day before and that he had come for a Polish Bible.

Mary was glad for the opportunity to witness to the inmates of the jail. But she would much rather help them before they reached that extremity. For that reason, the visitation in the saloons was always an important part of the ministry of the mission. This was usually conducted just prior to the evening street meeting. The pattern was to have two ladies visit together for their mutual protection and encouragement. After all, in the saloons they were really in the enemy's territory. One evening when Mary had marshaled her workers and sent them off saloon-visiting, she found she was all alone. Nothing daunted, she set out to wage the battle. She moved from saloon to saloon down Monroe Street, turned the corner at Halsted, and worked her way toward Madison. There she found herself in a little better neighborhood and a higher class of saloon. Inside, she was greeted by, "Hello, Miss Everhart! How do you do? I declare you grow younger every day." The speaker was a respectable-looking man seated at one of the tables. Minutes later another voice called out, "Why, it's Miss Everhart from the Olive Branch!" Mary knew neither of the speakers, nor anyone else in the saloon, but their friendly manner encouraged her to believe she was respected there, if not believed.

One time God laid one of the saloons on Mary's heart in a special way. It was the dirtiest, vilest place in the neighborhood. With great courage and faith in God, she asked the owner if she and her girls might sing a few hymns and talk to the men on Sunday morning. To her great satisfaction, he consented. So for a time, the mission workers conducted a weekly gospel service right in the saloon.

The saloons could not hold all the drunks. They overflowed onto the streets and into the cheap rooming houses. One Sunday as Mary and her helpers were returning to the mission, a drunk in the gutter attracted their attention. "Won't you get the ambulance?" he pleaded. "I'm sick, and I want to go to the hospital. Pray for me."

Two of the women went for the ambulance. One went for a glass of water. Mary and the rest prayed. Then the ambulance came and took him away. Later that week he appeared at the mission, sober and seeking further prayer and spiritual guidance.

Prayer was often requested, and given. In fact, it was

often given when not requested. One day as Mary was visiting from door to door, she was told of a sick young woman up the street. It was reported that the young woman was very hard and skeptical. Mary began to pray. As she got to the building in which the sick woman lay, she prayed with the family on the first floor. In her prayer she interceded for the sick woman on the third floor. This pattern was repeated with the family on the second floor. By the time she knocked on the third-floor door, the family inside no longer seemed like strangers. The young woman readily admitted that she was without Christ and was eager to have Mary pray with her. Several weeks later she was soundly converted and became a radiant Christian.

Door-to-door visitation brought Mary into contact with many kinds of needs — most of them related to deep sin and poverty. She sometimes visited a widow and her invalid daughter. The widow had to work many hours far across town. So, the little girl spent many days all alone. One evening, Mary stopped by on the way to the street meeting and left her own hymnal as a gift. The girl was delighted beyond description.

Another contact Mary made through visitation was with a girl-mother and her tiny baby. The mother was one of the inmates in a house of prostitution just a few steps from the mission home. One day white crape, denoting a death, appeared on the door of the house. Mary went to pay her respects and to pray with the young mother. She also felt she should attend the funeral service. But when the time arrived, no minister appeared. Mary and the workers who were with her offered to sing a hymn or two and pray. Their offer was gladly accepted.

Much of Mary's life was like that — simply being available and stepping in when the need arose. One evening, just at street meeting time, she spied an old couple hurrying toward her. The man was seriously lame in one foot.

Mary put them off until after the street meeting. Then she discovered they had been evicted by a cruel landlady. Mary took them to the police, who claimed they could do nothing. Then she went to see the landlady. The neighbors tried to dissuade Mary, predicting bodily harm. But Mary, not being the timid sort, marched right in. The landlady was unbending. So, there was nothing left to do but try to find someplace for the old couple to spend the night.

It was nearly midnight before Mary got the couple settled for the night. She spent the next day retrieving the belongings of the old couple from the hate-filled landlady.

One cold day Mary boarded a streetcar with her arms loaded with papers and tracts. She watched her fellow passengers to see whom she might help. Her gaze was attracted to a girl who was engrossed in a novel. Just before leaving the streetcar, Mary approached the girl to offer some papers and a tract. Out on the street, Mary was startled by the words, "I would like one, too." She turned to see a fine-looking young woman smiling at her. Thus began another friendship.

Several days later the new friend asked Mary to accompany her to visit a sick woman. Together they walked two miles through the cold, stormy wind. Their journey ended in a poor tenement house where, in a miserable room, an emaciated woman lay upon a ragged bed. She had once been a fine lady, the wife of a prosperous merchant. She had two lovely daughters, but her husband had become sick, and all their wealth went for doctor and hospital bills. Now the daughters were in an orphanage. Her husband was dying in a charity hospital, and she was deteriorating from sorrow, deprivation, and neglect. She had no one to care for her except Mary's new friend.

Mary was able to organize some of the woman's neighbors to help care for her. A girl was engaged to keep the fire going. Some of the women would bring hot food. In several weeks, the sick woman was again able to go to work and at least to care for herself.

There was no place Mary would not go in seeking those who might need her help. One day, while out visiting, she was told of a sick girl in a neighboring basement apartment. She searched and searched but could not find the room. She was about to give up when she met another young woman who could direct her.

Mary knocked on the door, far back in a dark corner of the basement. "Who's there?" a feeble voice inquired. Mary caught traces of a whispered conversation following her response. Finally, the door was opened, and she was hurried inside. In spite of the fact that it was a very warm July day, there was no ventilation in the room and no light except for two or three candles. The walls were bare. The only furniture was two beds, which took most of the floor space. The room was filled with a heavy smoke. Mary was amazed to find herself in one of the worst opium dens in Chicago!

The girl whom Mary had come to see lived there with a Chinaman who ran the establishment. Mary blinked, looked around, and burst into tears. With prayers and exhortations, she told the inhabitants, including one woman customer, of the One who is mighty to save.

Often after that, Mary returned to the opium den to deal with those she found there. Eventually, the police started raiding such places and that door was closed to her.

Some time later a young woman testified in the evening service at the mission. After the service, she approached Mary and identified herself as one with whom Mary had prayed in the opium den. The young woman had not been saved then. In fact, she wound up in jail. But the seed which Mary had planted bore fruit. Now the young woman was thanking God for His saving and keeping power.

Chapter 5

Holiday/
Holy Day

It was an hour before the meeting was to begin, but already the eager children were hurrying into the old mission hall. Their happy voices and quick laughter added to the festive air. It was Thanksgiving Day, 1902. Mary Everhart, Katie Hall, Mabel Lane, and the other mission workers had been working for days to give the children and adults a special treat.

Two days before, Mary had given up hope of receiving any chickens or turkeys from friends this year. Reluctantly, she had sent a worker out to purchase the needed birds at twenty cents a pound. Later that same day, some birds arrived by express. More came Wednesday. Now, when a childish voice would ask, "May I have some more turkey, please?" there would be plenty.

By 9:45 the hall was filled with about a hundred youngsters. The children seemed to forget the feast which was to follow and gave enthusiastic attention to singing, reciting Scripture verses, and listening. They were spellbound as Sister Wendell, of Chicago Second Free Methodist Church, told about her chickens. The birds were roosting in a large tree, and she wanted to get them down so they wouldn't freeze in the cold weather. The more she tried to reach them, the more frightened they became, and the higher up the tree they went. "Some people are just like that," she said. "When God wants to help them, they become frightened of Him and run away."

At the end of the service, a bright tin plate, loaded with good things to eat, was handed to each child. Most of the children had not seen such a sight since last Thanksgiving — and likely would not see such a thing again for another year. Yet everyone waited patiently until all had been served. Then they sang the blessing, and the feasting began in earnest. Later, each child was given a book, a sack of candy and nuts, and an apple. Then they were sent on their way home.

As soon as the children were gone, the adults were served dinner. The mission workers didn't stop to eat. They went right ahead with the preaching service. This lasted until late afternoon. Several persons found deliverance from sin. In the evening service, the Reverend Wilson T. Hogue, later a bishop of the Free Methodist Church, preached. Seven people responded to the altar invitation, and two of those gave clear witness to salvation. Following that, food was again offered to all who were hungry. Thus ended a busy Thanksgiving Day — and the weary workers could seek their rest.

Whether it was Thanksgiving, Christmas, New Year's, or the Fourth of July, the mission always had a good crowd. One time the saloon across the street offered a free turkey dinner on Christmas. The mission was still full. Sometimes such a large crowd was expected that the mission workers issued tickets. They were free, of course. But no one was to be admitted without that pass. One little fellow came without a ticket and was admitted by Mary only because his brother was to sing a special song. He was later converted and became a lifelong Christian and supporter of the mission.

Christmas was special because of the gifts. The workers were careful to provide presents for all the Sunday school children, the converts, and as many of the neighborhood families as possible. Many of the items were purchased elsewhere and sent to the mission by friends. For special cases, Mary spent precious hours shopping for just the needed thing.

One of those special cases was a dear old grandmother who often walked to the mission Sunday evenings wearing a pair of worn-out shoes. Mary determined to provide her with new shoes for Christmas. But that December, Mary was sick. She had to leave most of the Christmas planning to the other workers. Grandmother went without her new shoes.

Then one blustery cold day in February, Mary had to make a hurried trip downtown. These were busy days and she was rushing through many tasks, leaving many others undone. With her errands completed, Mary waited for the streetcar to return to the mission. She stepped into a store to get out of the bitter wind and spied just the right shoes for grandmother. Mary checked her purse and found she had just enough to pay for the shoes, with five cents left over for carfare. But would the shoes be the right size? That evening, before street meeting, Mary hurried over to the grandmother's home and presented the belated Christmas gift. The shoes fit perfectly!

In February of 1911, the mission workers asked Mary what they could do to celebrate her birthday on the thirteenth of that month. She replied she would rather have a good gospel service than anything else. So, they planned one.

Special announcements were made. Visitors went to every saloon and lodging house in the neighborhood with invitations to the great anniversary rally in honor of Mary Everhart. It was a success, and four men gave their lives to God that night. One was a white-haired old man. Another was a young foreigner who had difficulty understanding, but at last he grasped the truth of salvation by faith in Jesus Christ. A third was a poor cripple.

Every year after that, Mary's birthday was celebrated by a gospel rally.

Chapter 6

Wonderful Green Grass

"Now, children," the teacher asked, "how many of you have ever seen a real tree?"

Six hands shot into the air.

"Billy, where did you see a tree?"

"When you took us to Lincoln Park last summer."

What a strange conversation! Every child has seen trees, hasn't he? No, not if he was raised in the slum neighborhoods of Chicago. No trees grew near Olive Branch Mission. No flowers. Very little green grass.

For Mary, who had grown up in the beautiful farm country of Pennsylvania, the absence of living plants was a great loss. In her characteristic concern for others, she often thought of that loss in terms of the boys and girls around her. So, each summer she planned an outing for the children.

One year they went to the Lincoln Park Zoo on Chicago's north shore. One little fellow got so excited about the elephant that he fell right into the pen. He scampered out again through a small opening before anyone could help him. A little girl got lost from the group. When she was brought back by a policeman, she stayed very close to a teacher — for a few minutes at least. The children could not understand why they were not allowed to pick the pretty flowers. There seemed to be more than the park needed. One girl solved that dilemma by picking up a fallen leaf and asking if she could keep that. She treasured it as though it were a lovely rose.

Another time, the group visited Garfield Park. They were amazed at the vast variety of plants in the conservatory. Then there were the rowboat rides. Three boats had been reserved for their use, and the children clamored eagerly for their turns. After a picnic lunch, while they were enjoying a romp on the grass, El Joseph Raycroft arrived. This seven-year-old evangelist was the regular Monday night speaker at the mission. The workers called the children together and had them be seated on the grass. El Joseph and his younger brother and sister sang a song. Then the little preacher spoke about Jesus' feeding the five thousand. Before he had finished, a number of adults had stopped to listen, including two park policemen.

Another year, Mary determined to take the children to the annual children's day at the camp meeting at Glen Ellyn, twenty-two miles west of Chicago. It was no small job — herding forty energetic boys and girls that distance on public transportation. Most of the journey was made by train. They attended two meetings at the camp and still had ample time to explore their surroundings. Several children gathered bouquets of weeds, which they called flowers, and one spoke enthusiastically about climbing the "mountains." Another fellow was overheard calculating how long it would take them to tear down one of the "rag houses" (tents).

Some of the best outings they enjoyed were in Downers Grove. Mrs. Prince and some of her friends made all the arrangements. They even provided for free train transportation. All Mary and her helpers had to do was to shepherd the children there. Their first visit was in 1912. It was the first day of June, a beautiful day! Many of the children were already at the mission when Mary arrived a little before 9:00 A.M. There were more than forty children and six or seven workers. Mary lined up her charges, handed out one large flag and several smaller ones, and marched the troop the few blocks to the Union depot. Every green field and every cow elicited an excited cry from some member of the group.

Hostesses met the group at the depot in Downers Grove and guided them to the home of Mrs. Prince. There were three acres of lawn for the children's enjoyment. And directly in front of the house, there were three large tablecloths spread on the lawn. On the cloths were all manner of good things to eat. The large cups were for all the fresh milk the children could drink.

After lunch, Mrs. Prince's son Earl guided the group to a nearby woods where the children were allowed to play. One little girl slipped into the brook which flowed through the woods and reported to her teacher, "I got into the sewer." Then she asked, "Why do they have the sewer out here in the woods?"

When the group returned to the house, their hostesses served ice-cream cones and cupcakes. Then they sang a few songs and prepared for their return to Chicago. The day had been such a success that Mrs. Prince and her friends repeated the invitation every summer for several years.

Sometimes a friend of the mission would stop by and offer to take a carload of youngsters for an automobile ride in the country. Once in awhile Mary was able to send a child into the country for two weeks with a Christian family. She seized every opportunity to let the children see beyond the slums and behold some of the wonder of God's creation.

There were other times when Mary was able to get away from the slums for a while alone. As often as possible she made trips to various camp meetings to promote the cause of the mission. It was here she formed many of the friendships which proved so beneficial for her and for the mission.

It was Mary's nature to plan trips carefully. She did not believe in wasting time or effort. Thus, she would check train schedules and write ahead to be sure there would be someone to meet her. Even so, things did not always go as planned. Once, while chafing at an unexpected six-hour layover at Sarnia, Ontario, on her way to Sombra, Ontario, she thought she heard Satan telling her she had missed her way. But she was sure she was in the will of God.

When she arrived at Sombra, there was no one to meet her, there seemed to be no means of transportation to the camp, and the stationmaster was locking up the building. Mary discovered a farmer who was headed in the direction of the camp with a wagonload of lumber. He agreed to carry her luggage. Then she started out on foot. Soon a young man driving a horse and buggy stopped and offered her a ride. She arrived at the camp just in time to hear a sermon by the Reverend Mr. Height. His was the only familiar face in the assembly. Nevertheless, Mary enjoyed a wonderful and profitable visit with those warmhearted Christians.

Mary enjoyed the camp meeting trips. They were a

balm to her spirit and afforded a wonderful relaxation from the oppressive atmosphere of the slums. But they did not provide the rest for her body for which she felt such great need. From time to time God made a way for her to have special days of recuperation.

The summer of 1916 was particularly hot and stifling in the slums of Chicago. Mary felt the burden of the work more than ever before. Although she had arranged brief outings for all her helpers, she had not taken time off for herself — not even to visit the camp meetings she so much enjoyed. Then in mid-August she received an invitation from Mr. and Mrs. Samuel Garvin. They suggested she take the afternoon boat from Chicago to Ephraim, Wisconsin, at their expense. She could stay with them for several days and return with them to Chicago on their boat.

Mary's first reaction was to decline the invitation. But she decided to pray about it. The more she prayed, the more certain she was that God wanted her to accept. So, she sent Clara Spencer to the boat dock to purchase tickets for herself and Hattie Little, another mission worker.

The ticket agent laughed when Clara asked for two tickets for Ephraim. "Yes, I can give you tickets to Ephraim," he said, "because the parties that had secured a stateroom to that very town have just phoned us they cannot go. You can have their places." Then he continued, "The boat has been filled for weeks, and we have had to turn more than fifty applicants away daily."

When Mary boarded the boat Thursday afternoon, she ran into an unexpected problem. The deck chairs were so high her feet could not touch the floor. She was looking for something to use for a footstool when she spied one chair that was different. Someone had sawed six inches off the legs. It was just right! Of the hundreds of people on the boat, no one seemed interested in that one sawed-off chair. During the entire thirty-hour journey, Mary used it whenever she wanted it.

Her hosts met her at the dock, took her aboard their boat, and whisked her across the bay to a log cabin in a state park. There she enjoyed their company and that of several other houseguests for five days. Then they started their leisurely four-day journey home.

Mary reported that this vacation was "the most unlooked-for and most refreshing, restful outing of all the years."

Chapter 7

A Seed Sower Must Be Patient

So close, so close, and now he's gone! The young seaman had been attending the evening services quite regularly for several months. But he would not yield to God. Now with the coming of spring, he is returning to his rough life aboard a ship on the lakes. What will happen to him? Will he remain sensitive to the leading of God? Will he come back to Olive Branch Mission in the fall?

Yes, he did come back. But another winter passed without deliverance from sin. And another season on the lakes took him away from the preaching of the Word and thrust him among a most godless society for another nine months.

Again, he came back to the mission. On Christmas Day he surrendered his life to God and became a new creature in Christ. There were a few weeks for spiritual growth, and then he was off again to life on the lakes.

The next fall he could testify, "I have proved the grace of God sufficient to keep me. I know if He can keep me for one season, surrounded by drinking and swearing men, He can keep me until the end of life; and if He can save me from my sins and help me to live a pure life, He can do the same for others."

One evening following the service, Mary and several other workers were standing near the door of the mission speaking to the men as they left. One white-haired gentleman attracted Mary's special attention. He had pushed his way past the others in an attempt to rush from the hall. Mary spoke to him, but it was obvious he did not intend to be delayed.

Mary grabbed his arm as firmly as she could and fell to her knees. She cried out to God on his behalf. Soon the old man was on his knees with tears streaming down his face.

He professed himself too bad to be saved. But Mary prayed, and others joined her. Finally, he began to pray. His cries for mercy soon were exchanged for shouts of praise. He rose to his feet with a positive, emphatic testimony. He left that evening a new man, never to return to the mission. Where did he go? Did he remain faithful to God? Mary never knew.

Oh, the frustration of working with people who are unsettled. Oh, the heartache of having one's spiritual children whisked away. Satan often came to taunt, "Where are your converts? Where is the fruit of your labors? You have sacrificed everything, and what do you have to show for it?"

Once Jesus healed ten lepers. But only one returned to praise God. The other nine went on their way without a backward look. Mary often thought of that and asked herself, "Where are the nine" (Luke 17:17)? Then once in a while, one of "the nine" appeared.

One evening, when Mary was seated on the platform and the service was about to begin, a man came through the door, walked up the aisle, and took a seat near the front. Mary thought she remembered him. She studied him carefully and concluded he only resembled one of the converts. After the altar service, the man approached her and asked, "You don't recognize me, do you?"

"I've been trying to recall the name of the person I know that you resemble so much," she responded.

"My name is C____," he said, "and I was saved right here at this altar twenty-seven years ago. I have been out in the copper mines of Arizona for years, but I have kept true and have never gone back to my old life of drunkenness and other sins since I knelt here that night and found such a great deliverance. I wanted to tell you that the God who so wonderfully saved me that night has kept me saved all these years in spite of the awful wickedness around me."

One time when Mary was distributing tracts on Madison Street, an apparent stranger stepped up to her. "I have known you for fourteen years," he said.

"Are you a Christian?" was Mary's immediate response.

"Yes," the well-dressed man replied. "I used to be an awful drinker, but fourteen years ago I prayed in your mission, and I have never tasted a drop since. I have several thousand dollars in the bank as a result."

Mary urged him to return to the mission for a service. "I would like to," he explained, "but I am an engineer and work nights, so I don't have much chance."

Another time when Mary was distributing tracts, she was greeted with the familiar words, "You don't remember me, do you?''

She turned to face a cheerful young woman. With only an instant's hesitation, Mary replied, "Yes, how are you?"

"I am saved now, and so is Jennie."

Mary had first met the two young women about three years earlier. They had come into a service in the mission. Mary had immediately recognized that they were out of place there and took a keen personal interest in them. They confessed they were running away from home. Mary pointed out the folly of their action and persuaded them to return. She even accompanied them to the streetcar to be sure they started in the right direction.

A few weeks later, Mary received a letter from one of the girls confessing she had not told her correct name and address. Mary responded with a personal letter and an exhortation to seek God. The girls came to the mission several times after that. But neither showed any sign of repentance nor the desire to lead a life pleasing to God.

Mary lost track of the girls for a time. What a joy now to meet, with the good news that both were Christians!

How is it possible to continue a ministry to people with whom you cannot communicate? Mary found the answer — prayer. Many of "the nine," when they returned, gave credit to the prayers of Mary and the other mission workers for their steadfastness in the faith.

The mission family held prayer services at 6:00 A.M. and 7:00 P.M. every day. They also prayed together after every meal. Often the evening service ended with a lengthy season of prayer. Prayer was one of the most effective tools Mary and her helpers had, and they used it wisely and well.

The OLIVE BRANCH

THE WORLD FOR JESUS

ALBUM

Rachael Bradley, founder and superintendent, 1876-1893

Mary Everhart, superintendent, 1893-1928

Mable Lane, superintendent, 1928-1939

Katie Hall, superintendent, 1939-1952

Martha Boots Nygard, superintendent, 1952-54, 1967-69

C. N. Schumaker, superintendent, 1954-67

K. K. Ballenger, superintendent, 1969-74

H. T. Rasche, superintendent, 1974-present

Clara Spencer

Olive Branch Mission, 1978

Olive Branch Mission, 1978

1976 altar scene inside mission

Photo by Harry O. Sobye

Passing out clothes to the ladies

Passing out clothes to the men

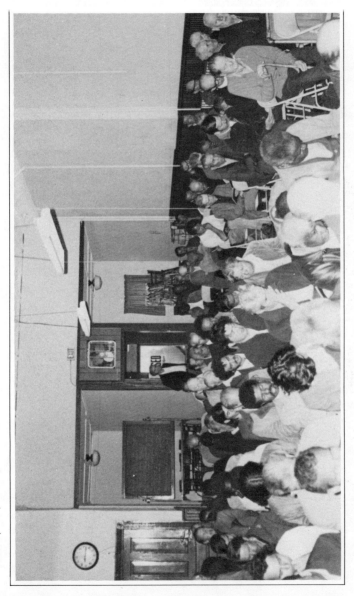

Photo by Harry O. Sobye

Mission service at Olive Branch

Mealtime at Olive Branch

72

Chapter 8

From Victory to Glory

"We can never get this hall ready for services this evening," one worker lamented.

But another with more faith responded, "By the help of the Lord, we will!"

It was Thanksgiving Eve, 1927. The hall was the new building for which Mary had worked, prayed, saved, and believed for many years. It was a happy, if busy, occasion. Services had been announced for that evening. The bare necessities had been moved from the old hall. Several workers were hurriedly arranging the chairs on the freshly varnished floor. Others were decorating the two fine display windows facing the street. Still others were hanging Scripture mottoes on the walls.

The only thing to cast a shadow across the event was the absence of Mary. At age seventy-four, she was no longer strong enough to participate in the work. She rarely had been well enough to attend the services for two years. But tonight she would be here, the Lord willing!

It was a good service. Mary was there. The Rev. J. T. Logan preached from Psalm 116:12-14. Among those who found deliverance from sin that evening were a young Scottish lad and a Mexican woman. The lad had hardly gotten his account settled with God before he wanted to write a letter to his mother back home in Scotland. The Mexican woman, before getting up from the altar, turned to a friend and her daughter who also were kneeling and exhorted them to surrender all to Jesus.

The new hall was located at 1047 West Madison Street. It was just six blocks from the Desplaines Street hall where Mary and Rachael Bradley had installed the mission in 1891. They were still within walking distance of all the places where they used to minister. But they were on Madison Street — the street of forgotten men.

The brick building had been newly papered when the mission purchased it. Mary ordered a fir wainscoting throughout to protect the walls from the expected rough usage. The partition separating the assembly hall from the kitchen was of the same material. Windows were installed the full width of the building at the top of the partition. This was to provide both light and ventilation. Later generations of workers would bless Mary for that foresight.

The mission owned this building. No longer would the workers need to dread the coming of the landlord to collect his rent. Now they were free to use the building just as the Lord directed. This was surely in fulfillment of one of

Mary's most cherished dreams. She had less than five months to enjoy it.

Over the years Mary had enjoyed remarkable health, considering the environment in which she lived. Most of her physical sufferings were the result of overwork, poor air, and inadequate diet.

Once in 1895 she reported that her right shoulder hurt so badly that she could not even write a letter. Four years later, she was stricken with a fever which brought her very near death. The workers called for an elder and had her anointed. Within thirty minutes she was sleeping quietly.

The report of her death in 1901 was premature. Her own response to that news was, "I am yet alive. Hallelujah! With God's help, I hope to do more efficient work for the Master than ever."

One evening in 1906 Mary prepared to go to the mission service. But weariness forced her to sit and rest awhile. Rested, she set out. At the mission, she forgot all about her own physical fatigue. Three people were saved that evening in a wonderful service. But back in her room, near midnight, Mary was seized with nervous chills — the result of her exertions.

In 1907 she was sidelined for eight weeks with illness. Three years later she developed severe eye trouble which was the direct result of the air pollution in the slums.

For years, Mary was troubled with rheumatism. The doctor attributed it to poor diet. He prescribed plenty of fresh fruits and vegetables. But how could a mission worker in Chicago's slums ever hope to enjoy that kind of food? Imagine her delight when she arrived at the Arnett home in Birchwood, Wisconsin, for a month's vacation in the summer of 1921. There she discovered more fresh fruits and vegetables than she could possibly eat. The change of diet and the fresh air helped for a while at least.

In 1922 Mary again came very close to death. Just

before Thanksgiving she took a bad cold, or so she thought. The cold did not go away but grew worse. There was so much work to do, however, that Mary would not consent to call a doctor or take to her bed. Finally, on December 3, she did both. Dr. Cotton pronounced her condition serious and asked for another doctor for consultation. Mary reluctantly consented. The diagnosis was congested lungs and weak heart.

The days stretched into weeks, and Mary's condition did not improve. Several times, even the doctor was about ready to give her up to die. Then on December 19, Dr. Cotton called the mission home to report, "I have prayed through and heard from heaven, and the Lord wants to heal Sister Everhart."

The next morning Dr. Cotton and the mission workers were with Mary, praying and thanking God for the healing which was about to take place. About eleven o'clock Mary felt the divine touch. An hour later she ate toast and a poached egg. She sat up for four hours that afternoon.

Mary praised God for healing her again as He had a number of times before. But there was a difference this time. Although healed, she did not regain her strength as rapidly nor as fully as previously. God spoke to her about slowing down and letting other hands carry more of the load. She was sixty-nine years old and had spent nearly thirty years in the slums of Chicago.

Her final illness lasted about two and a half years. She suffered terribly, but she did not complain. She repeatedly expressed her desire to attend the services at the mission, but just as quickly she relinquished even that into the Lord's hands.

Death came on April 3, 1928. The other mission workers were gathered around her bed. She lay quietly for some time, and then with an extraordinary effort she cried, "Amen! Amen!"

One of the workers tells what happened next: "We

propped her up with pillows, and though she never spoke again she evidently remained conscious for some time. She seemed to be looking at someone or something in the heavens, far beyond the confines of her curtained room. Only once, she turned her eyes to meet those of a worker who looked into her face. All the workers were gathered around her bedside, weeping and praying. Sister Winn was also present. Just about this time at the Free Methodist office, special prayer ascended to God for Sister Everhart, and one of the mission converts employed there poured out his heart in fervent supplication. As we waited by her deathbed, God also said, 'Amen.' The eyelids closed, and as Brother Adams had prayed and we had hoped, God gave her 'a quiet hour in which to exchange worlds.' When her gentle, loving spirit was caught away and the final change came, it was almost imperceptible. Sister Winn spoke, as soon as she could command her voice, of what was taking place in heaven and said, 'Can't you hear her shout? I can almost hear her shout her "Hallelujah" as she entered the eternal city and the glory broke in upon her.' "

In his tribute to her, Bishop Walter A. Sellew wrote, "The one great consuming passion of her soul was to help up those who were down — to rescue the submerged. This passion in her was remarkable in that it was well balanced between the humanitarian phase of assistance rendered and the spiritual uplift."

The Reverend J. S. MacGeary wrote, "Naturally a woman of refined tastes, the last place she would have chosen to spend her life, if she had followed her native instincts, was among the waifs and outcasts of society. But God gave her the vision of jewels to be dug from the slums, and she joyfully went down after them."

Mabel Lane was appointed the new superintendent of the mission. And seven weeks after Mary's death, the dedication service was held for the new hall on Madison Street. Bishop Walter A. Sellew was there to preach. He was assisted by the Reverends J. T. Logan, N. W. Fink, W. T. Loring, and T. A. Bailey. Two seekers responded to the altar invitation, and a Christian mother brought her infant son to the bishop for a prayer for healing.

Chapter 9

Her Star-studded Crown

During Mary Everhart's thirty-five years of leadership, Olive Branch Mission averaged one conversion a day. Well, you say, it certainly must have become a mighty institution with thousands in attendance. After all, any church which would see three hundred sixty-five new converts a year would become a great church. But mission work is quite different from church work. One of the primary differences is that the local church works in a stable community; the mission works with people who are on the move.

If people move away from the influence of the mission, do they still stay faithful to God? Mary wondered about that. She was so happy when she found a convert remaining true. But for many of her spiritual "children," she simply had to trust God.

Once a friend of the mission, Mrs. Mary Baker, returned from district quarterly meeting with this report. The meeting had been held at the Humboldt Park Free Methodist Church in Chicago. Mrs. Baker had talked with one pastor who was a convert of the mission. In the opening session of the meeting, four stewards from the local church distributed the bread and water for the love feast. Three of the four were converts of the mission. The wife of one of the stewards was also a mission convert. Reports like this cheered Mary's heart.

Those converts who chose to stay in the neighborhood of the mission found their new life challenging. More than once, a local saloon offered a reward of $10.00 to anyone who would draw a mission convert back into drinking. The reward was never claimed, as far as Mary knew.

Mary believed wholeheartedly in giving the new convert every support possible. The Sunday afternoon converts' meetings were invaluable. These bore some resemblance to the old Methodist class meetings. Only Christians were present. They talked, prayed, and studied the Scriptures together. It was here that many a babe in Christ was hurried on toward spiritual adulthood.

One of the early converts who sealed his eternal destiny by his death was George Bowman. George, born in England, moved to Canada when he was fourteen. Later he moved on to the United States where he took the broad way to destruction. It was on Halloween, 1899, that he found himself in Olive Branch Mission. But he was not like some of the low bums from the street. George was a self-assured, respectable man.

The invitation was given. Mary spotted George and moved toward the door to block his exit. His sneers would not budge her. Neither would his pleading. Finally, he dropped to his knees at the altar and sought God.

From the first, George was a radiant Christian. He joined Second Free Methodist Church but continued to come to the mission as often as possible. His happy testimony cheered many meetings and influenced many men for the Saviour.

Then George became sick and had to quit his job. Later, he could no longer attend the services. Mary found him in the consumptives' hospital in Dunning. Every time she visited him, he had someone with whom he wanted her to pray. His happy disposition made him well liked by staff and patients. He was quick to tell that Jesus was the reason for his joy.

George died two and a half years after his conversion. The mission and his church went together to provide for his burial. He died a pauper, not because he would not work, for he worked hard at a well-paying job when he was able. He did not waste his money on alcohol, tobacco, or gambling during that last two and a half years. George died destitute because he had gladly given away his money to anyone who had a need.

George Bowman had only two and a half years to live after his conversion. It was not so with Christ ("Chris") Simonson. Chris left his elderly parents in Denmark when he set out for America. He became a seaman and traveled for several years. Once his ship picked up the dreaded yellow fever from a port in South America. Chris and his bunkmate took sick the same day. Three days later, the other man died. Chris prayed with promises of reformation if God would spare his life. He lived, but he didn't reform.

Chris decided to try the life of a Great Lakes sailor. Perhaps he was attracted by the prospect of three months of wintering in Chicago every year. He began the winter of 1891 with a great drinking spree. Chris became sick from the drinking and went to his room. There he paced tho floor restlessly Then he remembered it was Christmas day. If he were at home in Copenhagen, he thought, surely he would go with his parents to church that day of all days.

He went to the YMCA, but they were not having Christmas services. Only then did he remember the little mission on Desplaines Street. The Reverend Mr. Kelsey preached straight to Chris's heart. When the invitation was given, he was quick to seek the altar and the God who can forgive.

Mary Everhart took the new Christian under her wing and helped him become established in the Christian way. He wrote to his parents in Denmark with the news of his change. As soon as possible he hurried to them, and together they rejoiced in the goodness of God.

For several years Chris lived in Chicago. He became a member of the Humboldt Park Free Methodist Church and a loyal witness at the mission. Later, he moved to Cleveland, Ohio, where he worked for his brother. He started a prayer group among the employees there.

Still later, Chris moved to Los Angeles, California, where he found work in the state school in Whittier. He felt a concern for the spiritual needs of the boys of the school. The supervisor finally gave him permission to take as many as three boys to Sunday school. Over the next five years, the limit was raised gradually until in 1919 he was taking thirty-seven boys to the Free Methodist Church in Hermon. That year he wrote to Mary: "Well, Sister Everhart, I will send you the picture of an old man who was saved in Olive Branch Mission twenty-eight years ago this Christmas. I was then a young man, but, thanks be to God, I am still young in heart. The Lord gives me great victory every day, bless His name, and it makes me feel happy and young."

Chris lived and served his Lord for another twenty years before he went home to be with Jesus.

There were ten rough, tough boys who called

themselves the Desplaines Street Gang. They were not the kind of boys who would attend Sunday school — not even a slum mission one. But one Sunday they decided to visit Olive Branch Mission for sport. They had not reckoned on the firm hand with which Mary Everhart ruled the mission. She put several of the ring leaders out, and the others followed until only one remained. He sat engrossed in a songbook. Suddenly, his face lighted up and he exclaimed, "Say, sing this 'ere song. We used to sing hit [sic] in Hengland."

The workers were happy to sing the song and even happier to find that their visitor could sing like a lark. He found song after song that he wanted them to sing. They gladly complied. When the session was over, Mary urged Harry to return the next Sunday afternoon.

Sunday morning came and Harry was with the gang as usual. About noon he excused himself to go tend his father's horses. With the task finished, he set out again, not to rejoin the gang, but to visit the mission. Again he enjoyed the singing. This time Mary asked him to return for the evening service to help with the singing. He was reluctant, but her power of persuasion was too great. He promised, and he came.

After the sermon that evening, Mary went to talk to young Harry Greenwood. As she spoke, others around began to laugh. Harry was stung by the laughter until Mary said, "They can laugh you into hell, my friend, but they can't laugh you out."

The truth struck home and Harry sought God that night. He found forgiveness and experienced a new quality of life. But he soon found the experience hard to keep. His joy had fled, he soon discovered, because there were some things which he needed to make right with people. He set about to do that, even if it took his last cent. With restitution made, victory came.

For years, Harry was in the mission nearly every evening. The music touched hearts and drew men toward the Saviour, whether in the mission or on the street corner.

Finally, Harry married and moved some distance from the mission. He still came when he could, and he always made a welcome contribution to the program.

What about Harry's old gang? Within a year or so, some of them were in jail. About twenty years later, Eddie Mac, one of the fellows escorted out the mission door that day, led one of the biggest and most daring bank robberies the city of Chicago had ever seen. He was caught and sentenced to a prison term. Harry was very conscious of the fact that, but for the grace of God, he too might have been involved in that escapade. Perhaps it was that realization that prompted the phrase, "It pays to serve Jesus," that was so often on his lips.

Space does not permit the telling of the stories of: The judge, William J. Devlin; E. Sharman, who was given charge of a rescue mission in Oakland, California, less than two years after his conversion at Olive Branch; Stephen LaPorte, who arose from the altar to surrender to the police and be sent to prison; August Beck, who was wonderfully healed; Henry M'Daniel, who had been in the worst kinds of sin for more than fifty years; Ole Aksalsen, who proved that an Olive Branch convert could "make it" in the United States Army; J. P. Berretta, who became a missionary to the Italians; Adolph Lidke, who graduated from Bible school and entered the ministry; and many, many more.

Surely there are many who will arise on Judgment Day to thank Mary J. Everhart.

Chapter 10

Faithful

It was camp meeting time at Byron, Wisconsin, when Mrs. Rachael Bradley spoke in an evening service. She told of coal and groceries coming into her Wells Street Mission on the wings of prayer. The lives of men and women were transformed by the power of God.

A young schoolteacher from Oshkosh listened enthralled. It all sounded so strange and unbelievable, yet she knew it was so. At that time Mabel Lane didn't even let herself think of what it might be like to work for God in such a place.

Several years later, in 1893, Mabel was teaching school in Chicago and visiting Olive Branch Mission when she could. But she had a "mission" of her own in those days. Although she was an active member of the Humboldt Park Free Methodist Church, she started an afternoon Sunday school in a large house in Palos Park. The boys and girls flocked to her until there weren't chairs enough for everyone.

Again several years passed by, and Mabel was back in Oshkosh as superintendent of the Free Methodist Sunday school. It was then that she heard a distinct call of God to Olive Branch Mission. She considered herself unworthy to be associated with the likes of Mary Everhart. But the call would not be denied. Mabel took up residence with the other Olive Branch workers in 1902. She was thirty-five years old.

Twenty-six years later, when Mary Everhart died, Mabel was appointed to the superintendency of the mission. Her apprenticeship under Sister Everhart had included many menial tasks. But, as Clara Spencer would say of her later, Mabel proved herself faithful in everything, no matter how small or how difficult. In her first years with the mission, she was given much of the responsibility for the simple household chores. Later, she took much of the work of the *Olive Branch* paper — setting type, keeping the mailing list, and so forth. She also learned to keep the books of the mission and spent many weary hours doing so.

In her early life, Mabel was timid and retiring. In later life she proved to be preeminently a peacemaker. Somewhere in between, was a period of self-assertiveness, coupled with a certain timidity, while she learned to express a strong concern for the welfare of those around her.

When Mabel assumed command of the Olive Branch, it had only recently taken up its new quarters on Madison Street. The mission bore the unmistakable stamp of Mary

Everhart. But Mabel bore that imprint too. Under her administration the programs of the mission remained about the same, not because she lacked imagination and creativity but because she agreed with the programs Mary had instituted.

Street meetings still spoke to the hearts of men and women who could not be persuaded to enter a mission. Children still flocked to the Sunday afternoon school. Slum families still depended upon the food and clothing which the mission workers could provide. The jail and lodging houses still provided places to preach the gospel to those who desperately needed it.

There were two significant changes in the ministry of the mission during Mabel's period of leadership. The first was good — Mary Everhart's long-cherished dream of a school for training mission workers became a reality. The other was bad — for the mission at least: In 1935 the Free Methodist Publishing House and denominational headquarters moved from Chicago to Winona Lake, Indiana.

From the very founding of the mission, friends connected with the publishing house and headquarters gave important support and encouragement to the project. Bishop B. T. Roberts, the Reverends S. K. J. Chesbro, W. B. Olmstead, H. L. K. Stokes, and Mrs. Mary Baker are only a few of these. Also, the publishing house and headquarters had drawn many others to Chicago, and to Olive Branch Mission.

The mission never had an official relationship with the Free Methodist Church. But it had been born within that denomination, and the two organizations continued to share a common spirit and objective. The mission provided a vehicle for the outworking of the strong social consciousness which the early Free Methodists felt. The denomination continued to figure largely in providing workers, prayer support, and material goods for the mission. The presence of the publishing house and headquarters so near the mission was a strengthening factor. That presence would be sorely missed.

The Olive Branch Mission Training School opened for classes in the fall of 1930, just two and a half years after Mabel became superintendent of the mission. Clara Spencer was placed in charge of this project. The school not only provided invaluable training for future missionaries; it also supplied the mission with a source of workers, both students and graduates.

Mabel gave thirty-seven years of service to the Olive Branch Mission, the last eleven as superintendent. She died on July 6, 1939, at the age of seventy-two, after a long and painful illness.

At Mabel's funeral three young mothers stood weeping beside the open casket. They looked with great love and tenderness upon the remains of the one who had been their Sunday school teacher in their girlhoods.

The funeral sermon was given by the Reverend A. J. Damon, who had been pastor of the Oshkosh church when Mabel was the Sunday school superintendent there.

The Reverend A. J. Damon once remarked that he was surprised when he heard that Mabel Lane was leaving Oshkosh to join the workers at Olive Branch. Mabel herself testified that her decision had been helped along by this poem by Katie Hall:

Your Work

There's work to be done for the Master;
  There's room in the vineyard for you;
Though much precious time has been wasted,
  There still remains plenty to do.

The fields are all white for the harvest;
  Wait not, lest ripe grain should decay;
Shall souls who might have been rescued
  Be lost while you fail to obey?

Oh! list to the voice of our Saviour
    Saying, "Tell all the world of my love."
Can you let them grope on in the darkness
    While you sing of mansions above?

Though you may not be called to the pulpit,
    Or over to some foreign land,
Tell someone that Jesus has saved you,
    And do the work nearest at hand.

It may be that some heart is longing
    For just the kind word you can give;
Then haste to deliver a message;
    Let someone be glad that you live.

It may be you have but one talent,
    But shall it be hidden away,
When, under God's blessing and guidance,
    It might become brighter each day?

When Jesus shall come in His glory,
    And Satan and sin be put down,
May yours be the blessed assurance,
    That no one has taken your crown.

Chapter 11

Sister
of
the
Bums

"It would have been a good thing if the Lord had taken her, too." The speaker, an old woman, meant well, but she didn't understand what God had in mind for little eighteen-month-old Katie Hall.

Katie's mother had just died. The heartbroken father was left to care for the two little ones as best he could. He eventually remarried, however, and provided his children with a fine Christian stepmother. Then, when Katie was nine years old, he also died.

When Katie grew to young womanhood, she went to normal school and became a teacher. But with her sisters married, she returned to the old homestead near Oakfield, Wisconsin. There she cared for her invalid stepmother and the farm on which she lived.

Katie became a Christian early in life. Her zeal for the Lord led her classmates to predict that she would eventually become a city missionary in New York. It is not surprising, then, that when she first heard of Olive Branch Mission she showed immediate interest. That was in 1894, and Katie was twenty-seven years old.

A married sister in Iowa sent Katie a copy of the *Olive Branch*. In response, Katie sent a donation to the mission. But even then she felt that the gift God wanted her to give was herself. She wrote to Mary Everhart about her feeling, and Mary wrote back in agreement. Mary was losing Lulu Howe in marriage, and Katie's lovely singing voice and talent at the organ would be a valuable help.

But Katie had a problem. How could she possibly move to Chicago and leave her invalid stepmother untended? Mrs. Hall, although a strong supporter of the work of the mission, could not bear the thought of giving up her dear companion and helper. Finally, a son-in-law invited Mrs. Hall into his home and the way was opened for Katie to join Olive Branch.

It was a big step from the peaceful farm in Wisconsin to the slums of Chicago. Katie went prepared for the worst. She left home on May 3, 1895, and arrived at Chicago's Union Station the same day. She carried a copy of the *Olive Branch,* by which one of the workers from the mission was to recognize her. Katie found the streets of Chicago not nearly as bad as she had pictured them. She was prepared to live in a shack and was delighted to find the mission workers' apartment bright and cheerful, at least when contrasted with her expectations.

Katie quickly fell into the routine of mission work, the work that became her life. Even on occasional vacations, she continued the work she found so enjoyable in the mission neighborhood. Her vacation in May of 1900 was typical. Katie set out for Oakfield, Wisconsin. But, having followed wrong directions, she found herself stranded in Harvard, Illinois, for nearly twenty-four hours. She didn't know anyone in Harvard, but that was no reason to sit idle.

Door-to-door missionary work in Harvard led Katie to a Christian woman who showed a great interest both in her and her work. After a pleasant visit, Katie made arrangements to spend the night there. Then she set out for more labors. She visited several of the thirteen saloons in the town, witnessing and giving out tracts. As she prepared to leave the home of her new Christian friend the next morning, Katie offered to pay for her night's lodging. Not only was her offer refused, but the lady insisted on making a donation to the work of Olive Branch.

As Katie resumed her journey on the train, she discovered a sick woman who also was going to Oakfield. She prayed with her and her husband and helped them in leaving the train in Oakfield. Later she visited the sick woman, and, after the woman's death, accompanied the husband back to the train for his return to Indiana. During the rest of Katie's vacation, she visited the sick, called from house to house, distributed tracts and papers, spoke in several churches, and attended a service in the state prison in Waupun. She returned to the mission rested, renewed, and ready for service.

In spite of her eagerness to be active in the Lord's work, Katie was not physically strong. Just two years after arriving at Olive Branch, she was stricken with tuberculosis. Her health failed from day to day until both doctor and friends despaired of her life. Her only hope, apparently, lay in fleeing the awful environment of the slums for better air and climate. She was urged to go to California to a married sister for at least a year. Even

Mary Everhart tried to persuade Katie to go for her health. In vain Mary told her that she would be of much more service to God well than sick. Katie's only reply was, "I am sure the Lord sent me to the mission, Sister Everhart, and He has not told me to go away yet."

In desperation Mary rebuked her, "Don't you know that they are blaming me for letting you stay?"

Gently Katie replied, "If I went to my sister's and knew I was not going to live, I would want to come back to the mission to die."

Satisfied, Mary no longer urged her to leave, nor tolerated those who did. God healed Katie right there in the slums. She lived to be eighty-five years old, working almost to the end.

There was something about Katie that set her apart from the other mission workers. It is difficult to tell just what that difference was, but it was somehow associated with the way in which she related to people. Professor A. E. Layman said of her, "When I began to hear of Olive Branch Mission some forty years ago and more, I heard the names of several persons. Those who loved them and their work spoke of Sister Everhart, Sister Lane, Sister Spencer, Sister Darling, Sister Harp, but never of Sister Hall. It was always Katie. So humble, so beloved was she that a formal name would not show how deeply they loved her." At the time of which Professor Layman spoke, Katie was about forty-five years old — the same age as Mabel Lane and ten years older than Clara Spencer.

One of the fellows from the street expressed it this way: "She's my sister — a sister to the bums!"

Under Mary Everhart's leadership, Katie learned the whole spectrum of duties associated with mission work. In addition to her musical contributions, she visited, preached, testified, wrote many letters to individuals and many articles for the *Olive Branch,* and superintended the Sunday school.

When Mabel Lane died in 1939, Katie was asked to

become the superintendent of the mission work. She was seventy-two years old. She tackled the new responsibility with her characteristic enthusiasm and optimism.

On a blustery March morning in 1943, fire broke out in the basement of the mission, perhaps started by a short circuit in the electrical wiring. Several workers were nearly trapped in the laundry at the far end of the basement as the flames and smoke swept toward them. Providentially, there was a trap door above their heads, and they scrambled through to safety. Firemen quickly arrived and brought the fire under control, but the damage from smoke and water was extensive. Katie and her helpers worked hard to get the building ready for services that same evening.

For Katie, as for her predecessors, services were not just to be "conducted." They were to provide opportunity for lost men and women to find deliverance from sin through Jesus Christ.

Edward Steeve had come to Chicago on his winnings from an all-night gambling game. His first night in town he set out to find another game where he could improve his fortune. Being a stranger in town, he started walking up Madison Street. When he reached the corner of Desplaines Street, he was attracted by a group of people singing on the other side of the street. He crossed over and listened. The music touched him, and the testimonies brought conviction.

When the crowd was invited into the Olive Branch Mission, Edward went on his way. Strangely, he was no longer interested in a gambling game. Instead, he returned to his room to pace the floor through the long hours of the night. Two days later he decided on a course of action. He deliberately went in search of the mission. He found it, went in, and listened to the sermon. During the altar invitation, Katie went to him and laid her hand on his shoulder, urging him to kneel at the altar and seek God. He did, and twenty minutes later he found complete victory.

Edward Steeve went out from that service to become a preacher of the gospel. He founded a mission several miles away from Olive Branch and ministered there for years. Special events often brought him back to Olive Branch to share his testimony and joy with his sisters and brothers in the Lord.

Frank Scheuermeier was also saved at Katie Hall's invitation. Frank had been born in Switzerland. He never knew his father. His mother boarded him at a farm and only visited him once a year. Early in life he learned to work hard. When he was fourteen, the farmer sent him to the coal yard to work. The work was heavy and his employer tyrannical. Frank didn't know how to pray, but he tried. His first prayer was for death. When that was refused, he began to pray that God would make him strong so that he could take care of himself. God answered that prayer.

At age sixteen, Frank struck out on his own. He arrived in the United States in 1923. He sought out the roughest companions. Soon his hard-won strength faded — the result of his wild life. It was a broken, discouraged Frank who stumbled upon the street meeting at the corner of Madison and Desplaines Streets in November, 1926.

When the invitation was given to come to the mission, Frank followed. During the altar invitation, Katie Hall exhorted Frank, "Young man, pray!" But he didn't know how to pray. He had never before heard there was forgiveness for sins. He wanted what the converts had, but he had no idea how to get it.

Katie led him in prayer and God gave some measure of victory. Frank returned to the mission several times after that. But Satan taunted him with the accusation that he didn't really know he was saved. One evening Frank went to his room, knelt beside his bed, and prayed from about 9:30 until 1:30 in the morning. Finally, God spoke real assurance to his heart.

For more than thirty years, Frank assisted in the mission whenever he could. His wife also proved to be an effective worker in the mission as together they labored for the Lord. In recent years Frank had made his home in Lawrenceville, Illinois, where his son, Paul, pastored the Wesleyan Church. Frank died September 13, 1977, still praising the Lord for His wonderful salvation.

Among the rush and bustle of her busy life, Katie found the time and contemplation to write poetry. Her poems started appearing in the *Olive Branch* about six years after she arrived in Chicago. For the rest of her life she was the "official" poet of the mission. Many of her poems were written at the specific request of Mary Everhart. In 1937 a number of her poems were collected and printed in a volume entitled *Gems of Comfort, Praise, and Victory.*

For the most part, Katie's poems dealt with the life of a missionary in a big city slum. But there was always a positive ring to the verses, because Katie was confident of the love and mercy of an almighty God. Many of her themes can be found in the following poem:

Wanted — a Worker

Wanted — a worker, true-hearted and loyal,
  Who fears neither cold nor the hot, burning sun,
Who counts it an honor to sacrifice comfort
  And thinks not of rest when the fight has begun.

Wanted — a worker who's careless of glory,
  Who seeks not for praises, for rank, or for gold,
His only ambition to build up God's kingdom,
  His greatest desire that the truth shall be told.

Wanted — a worker, a brave, loving worker —
  From every direction the call can be heard!

Wanted   a worker, the echo is flying!
Who'll carry the message — the life-giving Word?

Wanted — a worker right here in the homeland,
Where millions are dying in shame and in sin;
Oh, where are the reapers? The harvest is waiting —
Who'll bind up the sheaves and gather them in?

Calling, yes, calling — our own precious homeland,
Whose great, loving heart welcomes alien and son;
Oh, list to the cry of her millions now dying,
Send out brave soldiers; there's work to be done.

Wanted, yes, wanted — a worker of mettle,
Filled with God's Spirit, clothed with His might,
One who will stand when the foe seems triumphant,
Who conquers by faith in every hard fight.

Wanted — a worker who sees in the lowest,
Fair jewels of worth for the Master who died,
Who reaches a hand to the homeless and fallen,
And leads them in tenderest love to His side.

Wanted — a worker who cares for God's Zion,
And shepherds the sheep and the lambs of His love,
Who shields from the furious wolves that are howling
And guides to the evergreen pastures above.

On March 3, 1952, a lame knee prevented Katie from
attending the service at the mission. Her condition
steadily grew worse until she was called home September
9, at eighty-five years of age. Of the trio of long-time
workers who took up the load after Mary Everhart's
death, only Clara Spencer remained.

Even on her deathbed, Katie could not forget that she
was a missionary. Ethel Powell relates this story: "Just a
few days before her (Katie's) passing, a lady was visiting

here. I invited her to go in and meet Sister Hall, which she did. Soon after she was introduced, Sister Hall said, 'Pray for me.' The lady said, 'I don't feel capable of doing so.' Sister Hall then answered, 'Kneel here by my bed and I will pray for you.' The Lord gave Sister Hall extra strength to pray. I was standing by and felt so much of the presence of God, and I am sure the lady will never forget that earnest prayer."

Cameron McRae, a convert of the mission, wrote: "Sister Hall was a spiritual giant, and it is hard to worthily appraise the achievements of this great soul. But this we know, the world is poorer for her passing, and the cause of Christ has lost one of its greatest champions."

Chapter 12

The Last of the Trio

Clara Spencer had been at Olive Branch only a short time when she decided she ought to go somewhere else to work for the Lord. She even wrote three letters telling of her decision. Katie Hall took Clara aside and talked and prayed with her. The letters were never mailed. Out of that interview emerged nearly a half-century of service in Chicago's slums. Later, Clara would testify that she thought God had kept her at Olive Branch Mission because that was the only place where He could keep her.

Clara was born and raised in Milan, Michigan. When she was still young, her mother lay dying. "O Lord," the mother prayed, "let me live long enough to raise my daughter for You." He did.

After high school graduation, Clara taught school for three years. In those days she had many of the appearances of a Christian, even to the point of teaching a Sunday school class. But she knew her heart was not right with God. Then one summer day, as she was working in the farm kitchen preparing dinner for the workers, God said, "Pray." Clara glanced around at the pies and bread and then went to her room. There she surrendered her life to God and received a glorious sense of His forgiveness and presence. The year was 1901. Clara was nearly twenty-four years old.

In 1905, Clara graduated from Spring Arbor Seminary. Two months later she arrived at Olive Branch Mission. There she joined Mary Everhart, Katie Hall, and Mabel Lane. For the next twenty-three years, Clara served with these and others in the work of the mission. It was not until she fulfilled that long apprenticeship that she emerged as a strong leader in the work.

It had long been Mary's conviction that she ought to begin a school for the training of young women for the work of home missions. But as long as the mission was located in the old hall on Desplaines Street, there was no room for such a venture. Just five months before Mary's death, the mission moved into its new home on Madison Street. At last there was space for the beginning of the training school.

Mary appointed a board of nine directors and charged them with the responsibility of starting the school. She even made the laborious climb up a long flight of stairs to survey the rooms on the second floor. Yes, they would do; classes should begin as soon as possible.

Clara Spencer was appointed principal. She was admirably suited for the job. Not only was she a natural teacher and trained for **that profession, but she was** determined, resourceful, and energetic. She was a wise counselor. She had a never-quit attitude. Above all, she was a spiritual woman and a soul winner.

The school Clara helped found was different from most schools. There was no tuition. Students became part of the mission family and shared what the missionaries had. Teachers served practically without pay. The training combined study and practical work experience.

Teachers during the first years of the school included J. Paul Taylor, later a bishop of the Free Methodist Church; H. L. Crockett; B. J. Vincent, also to become a Free Methodist bishop; G. W. Saunders; C. N. Schumaker, later superintendent of the mission; J. R. Bishop; B. L. Olmstead; and Helen I. Root, former missionary to India. Later instructors would include such men as the Reverends Oscar C. Griswold, W. W. McCormick, Arthur D. Zahniser, and Robert M. Fine. For the most part, they were pastors who donated their time to the school.

The first class was held October 20, 1930, when J. Paul Taylor began a series on the life of Christ. In addition to mission workers, converts, and friends, there were eight students. The evening activities began with a devotional service in the prayer room, so designated by Mary Everhart. Mrs. Rebecca Sellew was there to give tribute to Mary's dream of the school. Helen I. Root was there to bring a short address. Clara Spencer wrote of that meeting: "God was with us in a marked way from the very beginning, but when we knelt in prayer, oh, how precious was the outpouring of the Holy Spirit. Never will this prayer service be forgotten. God put His stamp of approval upon the efforts already put forth and endued us with faith and courage for the future."

For twenty-three years, until her death, Clara led the school. It became indispensable to the work of the mission. Not only did it provide an enlarged staff for the mission through its students, but a number of the graduates stayed on as staff members.

Virginia Strait was one of those who found the training at the Olive Branch Training School valuable. She came from LaFarge, Wisconsin, at God's call. After completing the course at the school, she went to Spring Arbor to further her education. Then it was back to Chicago for nurse's training and on to Rhodesia, Africa, where she has spent most of the past thirty years.

Ruth Morris also took the training at Olive Branch on her way to a lifetime of service for God in Africa. There were many others who went out to be home missionaries, pastors' wives, or Christian homemakers and workers in their local churches.

Clara led the campaign to buy the building just to the west of the mission hall. The purchase was made in 1949. The three-story building eventually provided living quarters for training school students, classrooms, and much-needed expansion room for the growing Sunday school.

Clara lived with the students in the rooms above the mission hall while the other workers lived in the mission home ten blocks away. When the mission finally acquired a car, Clara became the driver. One day after she delivered the other workers to the mission home and returned to the mission, she saw a drunken man peering through the plate glass front. Clara parked the car, approached the young man, and spoke to him. He said he knew of Olive Branch Mission from his parents who had always taken the paper. Clara invited him inside. There she persuaded him to kneel for prayer. As she prayed, a training school student came down from her room on the second floor and joined them. Others drifted in and stayed to help pray. A convert was passing the mission and someone invited him to come help. The prayer and struggle lasted for about two hours. But finally the young man testified to assurance that God had forgiven his many sins. Several years later, Clara was visiting a camp meeting and met the same young man. He was a pastor and an earnest soul winner.

When Katie Hall died in 1952, it must have been a lonely experience for Clara. Though ten years younger than Katie, she outlived her by less than a year. Her death came on April 9, 1953.

One who witnessed the funeral service told this story: "Before the service began, many came to view her body. Among them was a very dirty drunkard. He came and knelt before her casket and prayed. A few minutes later he came back, and, with tears streaming down his face, placed one yellow iris beside her pillow. To me that was the most precious gift or gracious tribute that Sister Spencer ever received. Only heaven will reveal the results of her labors here on Madison Street.

The passing of Clara Spencer marked the end of an era. She was the last of the generation of workers who had received their training at the hands of the master mission worker Mary Everhart. Could the mission carry on an effective ministry in the tradition of Mary Everhart and those who followed her?

Several days after the funeral service for Clara, the evening service held promise of victory. But the meeting drew toward a close and it seemed that it must end in defeat. Finally, the last two seekers arose and left the hall without a clear witness of salvation. As the workers prepared to leave for the evening, there came a terrific banging on the door. Enna Bracken and other workers rushed to see who was there. At the door they found a young man with a troubled face.

"May I see the flowers?" he asked, pointing toward the funeral bouquets which still lined the altar. "I just love flowers, especially gladioli. I used to raise them in my garden back home."

They let him in and walked with him to the front of the room. There they urged him to seek God. He soon found faith to believe in Christ as Lord and Saviour. He admitted that before coming into the mission he had been so discouraged with life he had planned to commit suicide.

Yes, the ministry of Olive Branch Mission would survive the passing of the last of those three spiritual giants who carried on after Mary Everhart!

Chapter 13

When Martha Boots came to Olive Branch Mission October 10, 1933, Mabel Lane was still superintendent. Clara Spencer's training school had just begun its third year. Katie Hall, though sixty-six years old, still had nineteen years of service ahead of her.

Martha had graduated from Geneva College in 1928 and had taught school for six years before God led her to Chicago's skid row and Olive Branch Mission. That training and experience would prove invaluable in her thirty-nine years in the mission and training school. She graduated from the training school in 1938. Then for many years she taught the classes on teaching methods, church history, and English. Students who went out from her classes often spoke of the good preparation they had received for a life of practical service.

Over the years, Martha served the mission and training school in nearly every capacity — teacher, dean, principal, superintendent of the Sunday school, pianist, office editor of the *Olive Branch,* superintendent of the mission, and more.

Martha thrived on mission work. After a quarter of a century of service in the slums, she could say, "I can stand the work much better than I did twenty-five years ago, and I don't get nearly so tired." For relaxation on her days off, she liked nothing better than to go visiting in the homes of the poor people of the slums.

One time Martha and another mission worker were walking along together. They were several blocks from the corner of Madison and Desplaines Streets where the Olive Branch group usually held open-air meetings. As they walked, they spied a lone woman trying to start a street meeting. At her invitation, they gladly joined her and helped as they could in calling the lost to Christ.

When Katie Hall died in the fall of 1952, Martha Boots was chosen as the new superintendent. Two years later she stepped down in favor of the Rev. C. N. Schumaker. After his retirement thirteen years later, she again filled the post for a year until the Reverend K. K. Ballenger came as director.

Although Martha did not serve long as superintendent of the mission, she did provide a bridge from the leadership of that generation which succeeded Mary Everhart to the new leadership which followed.

In 1959, Martha received word that her mother was in failing health. Martha took a leave of absence, which stretched into three years, and hurried home to Beaver

Falls, Pennsylvania. There she cared for her mother until her death. It had been Mrs. Boots's express desire that Martha should return to Olive Branch Mission. That is exactly what Martha wanted to do.

When Martha arrived back at the mission in the fall of 1962, she found that a kind, quiet man had joined the staff. Herman Nygard had been converted in the mission about the time Martha went away. He was a native of Norway, where he had been raised in a Christian home. But when he came to the United States at the age of nineteen, he fell in with the wrong companions. Alcohol gained the mastery of his life. Try as he might, he could not break its hold. Finally at age fifty-five, he heard the gospel in the Olive Branch Mission and for the first time surrendered his life to God.

A little more than a year after Martha returned to the work, she and Herman were married. Together they continued on the staff of the mission until their retirement in September of 1976.

Chapter 14

In the fall of 1954, the board of directors of the mission asked their president, the Reverend C. N. Schumaker, to assume the role of acting superintendent. He would continue his pastoral work at the Free Methodist Church in Hammond, Indiana, and commute back and forth to the mission. Six months later the word "acting" was dropped and Pastor Schumaker had a new career before him. He finished his year at the church and then moved with his family to Chicago's skid row.

Mr. Schumaker was the first superintendent of the mission who had not come up through the ranks of the workers. But he was no stranger to the mission and its work. As early as 1932, he was on the volunteer faculty of the training school. At Christmas of that year, he brought his wife and two young daughters to spend the day at the mission. Six years later he conducted the consecration part of the commencement service for the graduates of the training school. By the time he was elected superintendent, he was president of the boards of directors for both the mission and the school.

C. N. Schumaker brought to his new job a wealth of experience from more than thirty years as a pastor, conference superintendent, and evangelist. He was a college graduate (Greenville College, class of 1923) with graduate work at Northern Baptist Seminary and the Winona Lake School of Theology. His wife, Alice, would prove to be an invaluable asset, as would their daughter Eileen. As a pastor's wife, Alice always had been interested in missions, women's work, and children's work. Olive Branch would provide a broad field for the exercise of those interests. Eileen was a hospital laboratory technician with an interest in writing. She brought a great deal of enthusiasm to many aspects of the mission work.

By the year 1956, the mission home on West Monroe was no longer serving its purpose. It had been purchased in 1911 to provide a safe, quiet, restful, clean home for the workers. But the neighborhood was no longer conducive to any of those things. The superintendent and his family, the training school principal and assistant, and the students already were living at the Madison Street properties. C. N. found that, with a little adjustment, all the mission activities could be placed under those twin roofs. The new arrangement made the lady workers feel safer, and it saved the time and expense of traveling back and forth.

For many years the mission workers had felt the need for space to house converts while they adjusted to their new life with Christ. Over and over, the workers lamented about how hard it is to send a newborn babe in Christ back into the old environment. Finally, in 1957, C. N. and his staff laid siege to the building adjoining the mission properties on the west. The owners didn't want to sell. The mission workers prayed! By December the owners were ready to surrender. The Christian shelter was about to become a reality.

The new building was a four-story brick structure, in nauseating slum condition. It cost the purchase price over again to get it into usable shape — and that with much volunteer labor. The men from the street were eager to help with the reconditioning. When the work was hardly begun, four of them were permitted to take up residence.

The shelter was operated family-style. Three meals a day were provided. Some of the residents had outside jobs and others worked around the mission properties. The "family" had devotions together at breakfast time. And they all attended the service in the mission each evening. This halfway house was a useful means of helping some men get on their feet.

Then tragedy struck! The building was inspected regularly by the fire department. Nevertheless, about eight o'clock in the evening of February 22, 1963, fire started in the basement of the shelter. All the men were in the service two buildings away. By the time the flames were discovered and extinguished, the damage was great. The building had to be torn down. C. N.'s first reaction was "Why?" But just as quickly came the assurance "God is in control!" Later it became all but certain that the fire had been set by a mentally sick man who had been living there.

Most of the men who were housed in the shelter had to be sent away. But several were kept to help with the clean-up. The lot was leveled and fenced. Grass and flowers were planted. That little twenty-five-foot strip of land became an oasis in the concrete jungle. Men would stand for hours gazing at the marks of beauty and love displayed there.

The human hurts and needs in the slums of a great city are almost impossible to imagine. One morning, as C. N. arrived at the door of the mission, a man was sitting waiting for him. "May I talk to you?" the stranger asked.

"Of course, come in," C. N. invited.

The old man, Jim, had been a successful man most of his life. Then he was falsely accused of a crime, convicted, and sent to prison. Fourteen years later his innocence was proved through the confession of the guilty party. The state gave Jim a large sum of money to make up for his wrongful imprisonment and set him free. But while he had been in prison his wife and only son had been killed in an automobile accident. At age seventy, Jim was homeless and friendless. His story told, Jim got up to leave. He had only wanted someone to listen.

Another busy day, the doorbell rang. It was an undertaker: "I have a funeral in my funeral home two blocks west of here. Could you be there in fifteen minutes and conduct a service?" Yes, of course, he would come. C. N. did his best to point the small group of mourners toward Christ.

Another time it would be a young couple wanting to be married, or a man wanting food, or a woman wanting clothing, or another man wanting two safety pins. The needs were varied. Some seemed trifling. But all presented an opportunity to act in love in the name of Jesus Christ.

The neighborhood in which the mission is located was never safe. One evening an elderly lay preacher was scheduled to speak in the mission. As he walked toward his appointment, two men confronted him. One thrust a pistol at him while the other grabbed him by the neck.

"Where's your wallet?" they demanded. As they began to search his clothing, an object slipped from under his arm and fell to the ground. One of the thieves picked it up and discovered it was a Bible. Hurriedly, he shoved it into the preacher's hand and resumed the search. They found the wallet, removed the money — a five-dollar bill and five ones — and dashed away down the street. "God bless you," their victim called after them.

Several blocks away, the thieves were stopped by a man begging money for a drink. The preacher, still on his way to the mission, came upon the scene and suggested half-jestingly, "Buy the man a drink, you've got the money."

One of the hold-up men stuttered, "If w-w-we'd knowed you was a Reverend w-we wouldn't 'a done this to ya."

"No, I'm not a Reverend," the preacher replied, "I'm only a lay preacher."

"W-w-well anyhow, d'ya want your money back?"

"Yes, I do."

Hastily, they returned all his money, escorted him to the door of the mission, shook his hand, and left.

C. N.'s beloved Alice went home to be with her Lord August 4, 1967. He continued as superintendent of the mission for a little more than a year after her passing. Then, at the age of eighty-one, he retired to LaPorte, Indiana, with his daughter Eileen.

Chapter 15

The Mission Man

In the fall of 1969, a mission preacher from the west coast was invited to Olive Branch Mission to give the sagging work a lift. He was to preach every evening for two weeks but continued for a month. At the close of the month of meetings, he was offered the job of director of missions operations. That is how K. K. Ballenger came to Olive Branch.

K. K., a rough-gentle man, had been a mission worker for twenty-five years. He had worked in the Peniel

Mission in Los Angeles, California. Before that, he had founded the Open Door Mission in Omaha, Nebraska, in 1944. Before that he had been a pastor in Nebraska. And before that? Why, before that — in Omaha, in 1935, God had saved him from a life of deep sin, at the age of thirty years. Almost immediately he went to work with the bums on the skid row of that city.

One of the first things K. K. wanted to do at Olive Branch was to provide a proper dining room for the men. Nothing fancy, of course, but someplace where they could sit at a table and eat their meals from a plate or bowl. Prior to that, meals had consisted of sandwiches and coffee served to the men as they sat in the mission hall.

K. K. convinced the staff and the board that by making some slight readjustments, the large room parallel to the mission hall could be converted to dining purposes. The transformation was made. As many as one hundred men could now sit down to a meal together. Now, when the service concluded, those who wished to pray could remain at the altar while the others went into the other room to eat. The plan worked well.

The next innovation for K. K. was the daily 5:00 A.M. service. He noticed that many men appeared at the doors of the temporary employment agencies by 6:00 A.M. They had had no breakfast and no prospects for lunch. How could they be expected to give a fair day's work with such a start? K. K. determined to invite them into the mission for a devotional service at 5:00 A.M. and serve a hot breakfast afterward. The crowd of appreciative men grew day by day until it was not uncommon to feed as many as ninety men. K. K. felt well satisfied when one man told him, "Reverend, I've never started a day like this before!"

Like his predecessors, K. K. felt the need to give housing to some converts in order to help them become established. He determined that even if he could only help two or three at a time, it would be worth the effort. So again there was some readjustment, this time in the living quarters, and space was discovered. The program was christened The Step Ahead.

In order to be accepted into The Step Ahead, a man had to give evidence of conversion. Further, he had to agree to submit to some pretty rigid standards. These men became like members of the family. When one fell from this position, his fall caused grief among the other members.

Fifty-five-year-old Larry was one who joined The Step Ahead. He had been on Chicago's skid row for twelve years. But when Christ came into his heart, his life was tremendously changed. For eight months Larry lived in The Step Ahead. Then he started spitting blood. "This might be cancer," the doctor warned as he ordered Larry to Cook County Hospital for tests. Fear gripped Larry as he remembered how several of his relatives had died of cancer.

All night long, Larry walked the streets of Chicago alone. He went to Olive Branch for a bite of breakfast and then started for the hospital. Along the way, an old friend offered some support from a bottle. Larry refused. Then a pill was offered. The temptation was too great. He didn't make it to the hospital.

K. K. searched for Larry all that night. For several months, all K. K. could do was pray for the missing man. Then one day, on the way to the post office, K. K. found him. The preacher urged the wanderer to return to the mission and to God. But Larry was evasive.

A few minutes later, on his return trip to the mission, K. K. again met Larry. This time the prodigal was more repentant. He went back to the mission and to God. How the staff members wept with joy as they clasped his hand and said, "Welcome home, Larry!"

Several months later a good-sized sum of money came to Larry. In his enthusiasm he celebrated in the old way — with alcohol. Soon K. K. was back out on the street searching for his straying brother. But Larry could not be found.

Holidays in K. K.'s ministry were important, as they always had been in the mission work. Christmas of 1970 was no exception. K. K. was scheduled to speak. But several days before Christmas he was taken sick. The other staff members weren't sure what was going to happen. But when it was time for the service to begin, there was K. K. on the platform. He preached as though it was his last opportunity. As soon as the altar invitation was given, men started coming. The altar was quickly filled. The front row of chairs was pressed into service. The men knelt in the aisle, and in the dining room. There were twenty-two seekers. And many found what they sought — deliverance from sin and the new life in Jesus Christ. After the service, K. K. returned to his sick bed and remained there for another eight days.

One summer Sunday morning the relative peace of West Madison Street was disturbed by the noise of breaking glass. A drunken fellow was shattering the plate glass windows in front of the mission. There were witnesses, and so police were able to capture the man just one block from the mission. A policeman warned the drunk, "When the men on West Madison Street find out it was you who broke the windows of the place that is giving them help, it won't be safe for you to step your foot on that street. Someone will get you!" Later, in court, K. K. refused to press charges.

K. K.'s heart sank as he surveyed the damage. The windows had been broken a number of times before. But they had always been covered by insurance. Now it was no longer possible to insure against glass breakage on West Madison Street. As he thought about it, he found a God-inspired solution — why not put up new wooden fronts with small windows? That is what he did, with friends of the mission providing the needed funds.

It was not uncommon for first-time visitors to the

mission to report, "We drove around the block three times before we spotted the mission." That is why, when the Reverend Carlton Rauch asked K. K. what he could do for the mission, there was a ready answer. K. K. wanted a sign that would identify the mission in no uncertain terms. Rauch said he would take care of it with the help of friends. The sign read "Olive Branch Mission, 1047-1051: Jesus Our Only Hope." The last were the very words Mary Everhart had wanted on a sign many years before.

Some time later, Chicago was whipped by the strongest winds K. K. had ever seen. He was pleased to see that the sign was barely disturbed.

K. K. was happy when two converts, John and Anthony, rented rooms less than a block away from the mission. They had been living eight blocks away. It had been hard for Anthony to accept Christ. In fact, it took nearly three and a half years of patient, loving interest to convince him that God really cared for him. His transformation was gradual as a new openness took the place of the former belligerence. Then there came a day when Anthony prayed and accepted Christ as his personal Saviour.

Only days later, the alarms sounded! Rescue equipment gathered at the apartment building in which John and Anthony lived. A faulty gas furnace had sent deadly carbon monoxide fumes through the second and third floors of the building. Ambulances carried away some who had been overcome. John was one of those; he would lie unconscious for twenty-two hours before recovering. Anthony didn't make it. How wonderful to know he had gone to be with the Lord he had served for only a few days.

After five years in Chicago, K. K. resigned as director of Olive Branch Mission because of ill health. H. T. Rasche, the present executive director of the mission, was appointed to fill the vacancy. It was October, 1974.

Chapter 16

God's Man for This Hour

"Here, Rev, you can have this. I won't be needing it anymore."

The Reverend Harold T. Rasche, the new director of the Olive Branch Mission, was pleased to see that the new convert was surrendering a nearly full bottle, not an empty one. But H. T. was even more pleased several weeks later to find the babe in Christ still sober and still rejoicing in his newfound faith.

H. T. had been directing the work of the mission for

less than six months, but he was no stranger to Olive Branch. He could remember back to Easter Sunday thirty-six years before when he had baptized four children in the mission. In those days he had been a young pastor in the Chicago area and took his regular turn in ministering in the mission. For the past eighteen years he had been a member of the board of directors of the mission.

In those intervening years, H. T. had served as a pastor in Illinois and Iowa. For six years his ministry had been extended nationwide as he traveled as a singing and preaching evangelist. He planned to conclude his active ministry after his retirement as assistant director of Woodstock Homes. But four years later, he was called to assume the leadership of Olive Branch. That was in October of 1974.

The Olive Branch Mission Training School had been closed for lack of personnel several years before H. T. became director of the mission. But H. T. and the board still felt a responsibility to help prepare young people for a lifetime of Christian work. The training available in a slum mission setting could not be duplicated anywhere else. To meet this need, they developed a plan for Christian schools to bring groups of students for periods of training.

Dr. Gilbert James of Asbury Theological Seminary was one of the leaders in this new movement. Groups also started coming from Greenville College, Vennard College, and Spring Arbor College. Sometimes the visit extends for a weekend; sometimes it lasts for several weeks. The groups range in size from one carload to thirty-five or forty students.

While living at the mission, students are given instruction to help them understand their surroundings. Then they are given practical experience in many aspects of the mission work.

Another innovation under H. T.'s leadership was the

creation of the service center. He decided to renovate the basement under one of the mission's buildings to make a reading room and facilities for shaving and showering. Here, men who wanted to escape the evil influence of the street could do so. The center would be open from 10:00 A.M. until 4:00 P.M. five days a week. This would provide excellent opportunities for counseling and supportive ministries.

Within days after H. T. announced his intention to create a service center, books and cash started to arrive, along with offers from men's groups in East Peoria, Illinois, and Griffith, Indiana, to remodel the center. In six weeks it was in operation!

One of the highlights of mission life under H. T.'s leadership was the centennial observance in 1976. The festivities came to a climax with the centennial banquet on November 5. The Reverend Dr. Clyde E. Van Valin, newly elected bishop of the Free Methodist Church, spoke on "Compassion — a Timeless Virtue." Training School alumni were present, as were converts and friends, old and new. Mrs. Julia Shelhamer sent her greetings by way of tape recording:

Words are too weak to express the joy I have in sending greetings to the supporters and workers of Olive Branch Mission in Chicago. That is my old hometown. That is where I got my first regular start in evangelistic work. I was then (1896) about seventeen years of age and had been called to preach. Sister Everhart gave me each Wednesday night to deliver a message at the mission. . . . I remember one night arriving at the street meeting just in time to hear young Harry Greenwood sing "A Lift on the Way." The chorus went like this:

> Then bear it in mind, to others be kind,
>   God's going to reward you some day.
> If a brother you find who has fallen behind,
>   Just give him a lift on the way.

125

That song captivated the whole audience, and I myself was thrilled with the prospect of giving my entire life to the happy work of helping poor lost souls enter the kingdom of Jesus Christ. . . . So, for eighty years, God has kept me busy for Him.

H. T. reported to the assembled friends that Olive Branch Mission, in its first hundred years, had conducted 71,000 public services; the workers had served 937,000 meals, given 323,900 garments to the needy, and distributed 2,800,000 pieces of literature. But best of all, 29,000 lost men, women, and children had sought salvation through faith in Jesus Christ.

As H. T. guided the mission through the summer of 1977, he felt an increasing pressure from Chicago's city hall. Years before, the city had warned that the area in which the mission is located was scheduled for urban renewal. That meant that once again the mission would have to relocate. When the mission had outgrown its first home in the basement of the Morgan Street Free Methodist Church, Rachael Bradley had moved it to a rented hall on Wells Street. When forced from there, she moved to another rented hall on Desplaines Street. The move to the present property on West Madison Street was made near the end of Mary Everhart's tenure. The painful search for new quarters had sometimes taken years. Now H. T. was being told by city officials that they had a buyer for the entire block and the mission would have to vacate within six months.

H. T. called for prayer, not only by the staff, but by friends across the country as well. The impossible happened — the buyer reneged! The mission would have a year or more to find a new home.

But where does a mission go? Will a move alter its ministry? One thing is sure — sin has not been eradicated from the city nor from the hearts of the people who live there. Wickedness gets just as much publicity and promotion today as it ever did. And evil still traps and destroys people by the hundreds every day. The work must go on, for the need goes on!

So, at Olive Branch Mission, the light still shines.